The Planning game
by Ken Dijksman

The Planning game

How to win planning permission

Ovolo Publishing
1 The Granary
Brook Farm
Ellington
Huntingdon
Cambridgeshire
PE28 0AE

01480 891777

First published March 2007
Revised edition January 2008

Special thanks to Anna Thompson FRICS FBEng Chartered
Building Control Surveyor for the building regulations
revisions in this edition.

Contact Ken Dijksman at: dijksman@msn.com

Title and this edition © Ovolo Publishing Ltd 2007 and 2008
Main text © Ken Dijksman 2007
ISBN: 978-0-9548674-1-6
Cover design: Gill Lockhart
Illustrations: BHP Harwood Architects, 01235 764166 (unless stated)

Printed in Great Britain by Biddles Ltd, King's Lynn, Norfolk

The Planning game

INSIDE:

Contents

The Planning Game

1

Chapter 4

Extensions   47

Contents

The Planning Game

Chapter 5
Planning for newbuild   71

2

Chapter 6
Tricks of the trade   95

Contents

The Planning Game

3

Chapter 9
Avoiding a refusal   **135**

Contents

The Planning Game

4

Contents

The Planning Game

5

How to object to an application   **203**

Frequently asked questions   **207**

Glossary of planning terms   **221**

Chapter 1

INTRODUCTION

As a developer, self-builder, home improver or property investor you need to understand how to get, or avoid the need for, planning permission. It is the key that unlocks the value of land. Agricultural land is worth about £3000 an acre but with permission for residential development that same acre can be worth up to £2 million. But there is no shortage of land, just look at any part of the UK from the air and it is astonishing just how green and undeveloped our small island is. It's not the land that we are short of; it's the planning permissions that are in short supply.

Achieving a basic knowledge of how the system is supposed to work is not difficult but neither is it enough to give you the edge. Making the most of planning opportunities requires an understanding of the processes and culture of local government decision-making, the details and subtleties of the legal background and the dynamics of local politics. You need to be able to distinguish between irrelevant detail and vital nuggets of information because they can look very similar. An understanding of the jargon is essential to enable you to make sense of the policies and to talk to planners in their own obscure language. Planning is, above all, a game of tactics and timing that requires a clear grasp of the constraints under which the other side is forced to operate. An understanding of the psychology that dominates local government enables loopholes to be exploited and maximises the chances of getting that valuable planning permission.

Nationalisation of development rights

Before 1947 there was no such thing as a modern-day town planning. If you owned land then you were pretty much free to do whatever you liked with it and to build whatever you liked on it. But in a post-war world of bomb sites and ribbon development the new socialist government effectively nationalised the right to develop the most important economic and social resource available to the country, land.

Ironically this initially socialist system of control has become the darling of the property owning classes, keen to protect their investments and prevent change. Since 1947 getting planning permission for any kind of development has become progressively less straightforward, less predictable and more political. People who are new to property development talk about building in accordance with the rules or complying with the regulations. In the world of planning there are no transparent rules or regulations and it can be very hard to predict what might actually be allowed. This is because planning is not about clear and easily understood regulations, it's a game. Like any game there are rules that govern how you play it, but not who wins. And in planning the referee is rarely if ever impartial. Regardless of the scale of your development it is a game of local (sometimes national) politics micromanaged by bureaucrats, so success depends upon how well you present your case and how effectively you can influence public opinion and persuade the decision-makers to let you win.

Rules of the game

The rules of this political game are written and administered by local bureaucrats acting on behalf of their political masters. The main aim of the national and local politicians is to avoid upsetting anybody whilst maintaining their support and balancing competing interests. Because developing land is at the heart of everything, socially, economically and environmentally, it is quite convenient to be able to hide behind the word planning instead of politics. It is even more convenient to consult everybody about everything so that the decisions that are eventually made have the notional stamp of public involvement and democratic approval. The policies governing planning decisions exist at national, regional, county and district level. Each level produces policy documents and employs bureaucrats who need to justify their existence and progress their careers. The game is to understand which planning policies are the most relevant and important and then either influence what the policies actually say or how they are interpreted and ultimately to persuade the local elected councillors and or their officers of the acceptability of a particular development. Whether you are seeking to build one house or 50 houses or a small extension, the same basic process will apply. There are planning policies that you have to work within or around and that you can use to justify what you intend to do but only if the local planners and politicians accept your arguments.

Contradictory public attitudes to development

The great British public appears to suffer from a range of reasonable but contradictory aspirations. People would generally like to own a house with a garden in a nice location. But people do not want any more houses built in nice locations because it is feared that will spoil them. People would like their children to be able to get onto the property ladder at a reasonable price but the same people do not want land made available for housing because they fear 'concreting over the countryside'. The reality is that the vast majority of the British countryside is inaccessible and privately owned and drenched in pesticides and herbicides, denuded of wildlife and generally raped by intensive factory farming. Thousands upon thousands of miles of hedgerow have been removed since the Second World War and all manner of wildlife is in serious decline. Yet this is the agri-desert the great British public is terrified of losing. It seems that excessive mortgages, tiny houses, small gardens and delayed home ownership are considered to be a price worth paying for its protection. Albeit that the amount of land required to be released to bring housing supply more in line with demand is proportionately very, very small. According to the Campaign for the Protection of Rural England only about 10 per cent of this country's land area is actually currently developed. The fear of new housing as propagated by pressure groups is consigning huge numbers of younger people to small, overpriced houses because of artificially high land values. Meanwhile our precious towns and large villages are becoming ever more crammed with intensively developed areas. But apparently that's okay because there is no Campaign for the Protection of Urban England.

The Government's planning body, the Department of Communities and Local Government gives an overview of the planning system that starts, "England is one of the most crowded countries in the world. Over 90 per cent of our population lives in urban areas covering just eight per cent of the land area." In other words our planning policies compress people onto less than 10 per cent of the available space, thus creating an overcrowded living environment and a serious shortage of houses. It's got nothing to do with the size of the country, the overcrowding problem is a function of prioritising the preservation of agricultural land above the quality of life of the bulk of our population. The irony is that houses are actually astonishingly cheap to build and it's the land price alone that pushes them out of reach of many of the low-paid. In accordance with the contradictory desires of the British people, the culture and ethos of the planning system is essentially negative and anti-development.

Difficult politics

In any planning decision somebody wins and somebody loses and local politicians have volunteered for the uncomfortable job of making that decision. Because most people do not like change, politicians almost always see planning approvals as vote losers not vote winners. Only in economically disadvantaged locations will planning permissions usually be welcomed. This means that generally speaking politicians look for ways to avoid being held accountable for controversial new developments. Massive public consultation exercises help to defuse blame and pointing the finger at the professional planning officers can be a useful escape route. If all else fails the local politicians can simply ignore the advice of their professional bureaucrats and refuse an application. The decision then passes to the independent Planning Inspectorate which makes a decision based on compliance with the relevant national and local planning policies. Politicians quite like planning appeals as they get them off the hook and the local papers can still claim that they 'fought it all the way' only for it to be allowed at appeal. Blaming central government like this is also normally good politics, particularly if different parties are involved. The result of all this is the painfully slow process necessary to get planning permission. Recent government rearrangements in the processes at the local level are only likely to make the whole thing even slower.

The answer is no

English law was once underpinned by the notion that citizens are free to do as they wish unless there is a specific reason why they shouldn't. This contrasts with the continental approach of being free to do only what the state will let you do. Planning has moved from the former to the latter. Because local planners have nervous political masters who don't like unpopular decisions, and because planning is essentially a reactive and restrictive exercise, the whole culture of local authority planning departments is antidevelopment and profoundly negative. The name given to the sections that deal with planning decisions is usually Development Control, although Development Prevention would probably be more apt.

Planning officers are usually driven by good intentions and have a sincere belief in the public interest and their own professionalism. Most of them would also genuinely like to be helpful. Unfortunately, the system within which they work generally rewards a negative process-based mindset. It is a sad fact that in a bureaucratic system, careers depend upon creating not solving problems; the more complex the task the more people are needed to do it, greater are the rewards for those who do. So it is always in the interests of local government officers to advance their status in the eyes of their managers by demonstrating how thorough they are in identifying new problems. The concept of receiving a planning application and simply approving it without any interference is an anathema to this mindset. No planning officer ever got into trouble for saying no. They risk getting into trouble for being too positive, too helpful and actually trying to work with an applicant to find a solution. This is because development is seen as a bad thing and the local politicians do not want their planning officers going around encouraging it!

Targets

The Labour government's obsession with targets has created a process-driven climate in which ticking boxes is rewarded regardless of the quality of the decisions or experiences of the people involved. Therefore, a quick decision is a good decision, regardless of whether it wastes an inordinate amount of the applicant's time or results in a poor quality of development. The net result of the targets culture has been to extend the length of time it takes to work through the planning maze; cleverly, the targets just measure the bit during which a planning application is actually processed; ignoring all necessary pre-application discussions, negotiations, investigations, consultations and all post-permission submissions. And there is, of course, no box to tick for spending valuable time just being helpful.

Local authorities' admin teams are, of necessity, becoming expert in the art of operating this system. It is an art in itself to reject planning applications prior to registration for some minor omission or transgression of petty rules, most of which have been imposed by the government who reward such attitudes. As a real life example, a fellow consultant recently had his application for the siting of a cashpoint machine in the wall of a building returned to him. The reason given that the (in this case wholly pointless) Design and Access Statement that accompanied it had omitted to deal with the issue of landscaping.

Too much power

There is also the problem of too much power and a delight in using it for its own sake. Planners have an enormous amount of influence and can cost developers and hapless homeowners, huge amounts of money through delays and needless interference in the trivia of development proposals. This is with the blessing of increasingly interventionist micromanagement from above. So very junior inexperienced planning officers, the kind who get the bum job of having to deal with the public, often feel the need to interfere and negotiate on proposals for the sake of it. They do not feel that they're doing their job if they just say, "Yes, that looks fine." Because of the longstanding anti-development culture developers and property owners are more or less considered by the system to be the enemy, motivated by that evil thing called money. So there can be a certain moral righteousness amongst some planning officers who see it as their sacred duty to reduce the size, scale, extent and viability of almost any development proposal.

The language of planning and design

Planning documents are riddled with jargon and planning policies have their own language which is often ultimately ambiguous and subjective. The same phrases crop up again and again, used to justify what planners would like to see and to justify reasons for refusal. A classic phrase is that development should be 'in keeping, with the character of the area'. The interpretation of which is very much down to the decision maker. Another very common phrase is that development should incorporate a 'high quality of design'. This is not dissimilar to saying that a work of art should be of a high quality; in other words they have to like it. Ask three planners their opinion of the design of a building and you are likely to get three different answers.

An awful lot rests on the subjective op   of the person empowered to make a judgment and there is an implicit assumption that planners themselves have some special understanding of words and phrases like 'quality', 'in keeping', 'fitting in', 'local character', 'over-development', 'incongruous', 'obtrusive in the street scene' etc. The reality is that these phrases are used simply to put the applicant, private individual or developer on the defensive so they are force   ut a case in favour of what they wish to build in highly subjec   which can of course be readily contradicted.

In my experience, subjective arguments are the ultimate escape route for any planning committee that would like to refuse a development, sometimes contrary to their officers' recommendation, because of local opposition. They can almost always argue that a development will be out of keeping with the character of the area. Because of the hugely subjective nature of this accusation a half reasonable planning argument can almost always be found to support such aesthetic and ephemeral opinions.

Despite being expected to make daily judgements on the acceptability of architectural solutions, very few practicing local authority planning officers have any significant design training comparable to an architect or fully qualified urban designer. As a result, when assessing the acceptability of a development in these terms, they end up applying familiar rules of thumb and development control standards enshrined in their authorities' supplementary planning guidance. Beyond this they either rely on their own personal taste or the views of colleagues or by simply trying to ensure that a development looks like, and is about the same size as, its neighbours. The latter approach is always safe and can be easily explained and is consistent with professional planners' concerns about context. But it is not an effective way of vetting and controlling extremely expensive and carefully conceived development proposals.

It is usually politically expedient to be conservative in matters of architectural design because local politicians know full well that the public have been scarred by the memories and experiences of 1960s brutalist architecture. Neo-vernacular, neo-Georgian or Tudorbethan designs all sit more comfortably with local public opinion than contemporary approaches. Left to their own devices many developers would also choose very traditional design solutions but then suffer from criticisms about mediocrity and lack of adventurous architecture from the very same authorities that object to modern designs. Not an easy battle to win with so many contradictory influences.

The tension between nostalgic and comfortable images of old England and the self-conscious modernist approach is reflected in local and national government policies, which applaud the latest energy-saving technologies whilst also seeking to ensure that developments respect local traditions and sense of place. Trying to button-down what that means in practice normally results in a standard palette of Victorian or Georgian-inspired architecture with a few modern elements thrown in, plus materials that pay some lip service to whatever styles can be identified amongst the local, usually standard 19th-century, building types.

Whilst accepting that subjective judgments and opinions have to be dealt with when approaching a planning problem, it is also worth remembering the kind of language that planners do not respond well to. They generally react badly to anything to do with money. The planning system has at its core the notion of the public interest overriding the private purse. So claiming the needs of poverty or profit rarely helps. Personal circumstances, however genuine and heartrending, are not normally a material planning issue and are very unlikely to touch the hearts of the average planning officer who hears a thousand good reasons every day as to why particular individuals should be given some sort of special treatment. A lot of objectors to planning proposals know this and shield their fears of property devaluation behind the full range of planning policy jargon.

The major developers, whose interests are not tackled or intended to be covered by this book, approach the problem of subjectivity and design by employing armies of consultants. They seek to button-down every possible concern by having a well-qualified expert to give confident pronouncements in advance of the planning officer's possible objections. They out-expert the local authority so that no one is in any doubt that any future planning appeal will be both major and expensive. This tactic, when coupled with shrewd political positioning, can be very effective but is normally the preserve of those with extremely deep pockets.

Opportunities

If this all sounds rather negative, it is because planning is not easy. But the difficulties of getting planning permission also create opportunities for making money. The scarcity of land with permission means that, by knowing how to play the game, land values can be transformed. Because planning is unpredictable and political, it is also surprisingly flexible. As policies change and local priorities evolve sites that were once out of favour can become ripe for development and equally locations which may have had real development potential in the recent past, can suddenly become worthless.

The opportunities to be found in playing the planning game exist in the short, medium and long-term. They do not even necessarily require the ownership of land, just the ability to make deals and establish option arrangements to buy land subject to successfully getting permission. In the long-term, sites can be promoted through the local planning process, so eventually they become allocated for industrial or residential development. In the medium-term, difficult sites that arguably conform to local planning policies can be pursued through the planning appeal mechanism. In the short-term, planning applications can be submitted to get permission and add value.

Chapter 2
AN OVERVIEW

What is planning permission?

Planning permission allows for the development of land and existing properties and is usually granted by the local planning authority (part of the local council). Planning permission is necessary because various town and country planning acts require local authorities to control what can be built, and how buildings and land are used. Planning permission is applied for by using particular forms and plans and it is granted or refused in writing by the relevant local planning authority. The permission runs with the land and is rarely personal to the applicant.

What is the difference between full & outline permission?

Planning permission can be granted in two forms; firstly as a full detailed consent, which includes all the necessary plans and drawings for the local authority to understand and specify exactly what is being granted. The second is known as outline permission and this is split into two parts - the outline permission itself, which contains limited information, and the subsequent reserved matters submission that fills in all the gaps and provides the remaining drawings. The outline permission, plus the reserved matters, provides the same information that would be submitted in a full detailed application.

Until recently an outline planning application could be a very simple thing, involving no more than a red line on a location plan and a broad description of what was intended, something as simple as 'residential development'. This was a cheap and effective way of establishing the principle of developing land so that it could then be sold on and someone else would then tackle the detailed issues. These historic outline permissions still exist and remain in force until they expire.

Outline applications remain in name but in reality the amount of information now required is barely distinguishable from a full detailed proposal.

Outline planning permission

An outline application does not need to include the designs of the proposed buildings but it must include information about the use and amount of development, including a basic level of information, such as indicative plans showing the layout, scale and site access.

As a minimum, therefore, the government specifies that such applications should always include information on:

Use – the use or uses proposed for the development and identifying any distinct development zones within the site

Amount of development – the amount of development proposed for each use in square metres.

Indicative layout – an indicative layout with separate development zones proposed within the site boundary where appropriate.

Scale parameters – an indication of the upper and lower limits for height, width and length of each building within the site boundary.

Indicative access points – an area or areas in which the access point or points to the site will be situated.

This amount of information can only really be derived from a scheme that has been almost completely designed, so the difference between an outline and detailed application is probably going to be marginal. It is only really the detailed design of the houses and landscape layouts that will be omitted. The system is so new that it is not clear yet how it will pan out in practice.

Design and Access Statements accompanying an outline application
The government now requires that Design and Access Statements accompany an outline application and to quote government advice they: must explain how the applicant has considered the proposal, and understands what is appropriate and feasible for the site in its context. It should clearly explain and justify the design and access principles that will be used to develop future details of the scheme. Such information will help community involvement and informed decision making. The Design and Access Statement will form a link between the outline permission and the consideration of reserved matters.

Reserved matters

The submissions made following the granting of outline permission - the reserved matters - used to consist of siting, design, external appearance, means of access and the landscaping of the site. You will still come across planning permissions in this format.

Recent changes revised this so that reserved matters are now:

Layout – the way in which buildings, routes and open spaces are provided within the development and their relationship to buildings and spaces outside the development.

Scale – the height, width and length of each building proposed in relation to its surroundings.

Appearance – the aspects of a building or place which determines the visual impression it makes, excluding the external built form of the development.

Access – the accessibility to and within the site for vehicles, cycles and pedestrians in terms of the positioning and treatment of access and circulation routes and how these fit into the surrounding access network.

Landscaping – the treatment of private and public space to enhance or protect the site's amenity through hard and soft measures, for example, through planting of trees or hedges or screening by fences or walls. Information to be submitted with an outline application

Is planning permission always required?

There is a wide-ranging list of developments that do not require the explicit grant of planning permission. This list includes development by telecoms operators, government departments, the Highways Agency, airport operators and farmers. These developments are known, for obvious reasons, under the collective title as permitted development. These large scale rights do not generally concern the small developer or investor but they can be extremely useful in major developments by statutory bodies and by farmers.

In relation to private houses, there are a range of alterations and structures that may be built onto a house or garden which do not require planning permission. These domestic permitted development rights can only be used once and if a planning permission for extensions is implemented before the permitted development is used up it will be lost. So always try and take advantage of permitted development rights before putting into effect any planning permission. Unless, of course, the permission is for a new house in which case the permitted development rights only become available once the house is complete.

The government is threatening to review, update and generally simplify permitted development rights across the board. But on its past record this will probably mean a significant reduction in the rights of individuals and the introduction of greater complication and delay through greater bureaucratic involvement. In Scotland these domestic permitted development rights are set out slightly differently than in England and Wales, being measured in square metres rather than cubic metres.

Permitted development rights in England and Wales are explained more fully in Appendix I.

What does planning permission control?

Planning permission is a distinct regime with its own legally defined boundaries, it can control:

■ The erection, location, appearance, use and occupation of proposed new buildings
■ Changes in the appearance and size of existing buildings
■ Changes in the use and occupation of existing buildings or land

What does planning permission not control?

■ Planning permission does not concern itself with how a building is built. A separate system of building regulations is involved. But it is increasingly being directed towards the incorporation of environmentally friendly design considerations, accessibility issues and security concerns

■ Planning permission does not affect property ownership or other legal interests or covenants relating to property. Planning permission can be granted on land not in the ownership of an applicant, the fact of the grant permission does not of itself affect other pre-existing property rights

You can access the latest government planning information, local authority websites and download planning application forms, appeal forms and work out what your planning permitted development rights are at the government's own site, www.planningportal.gov.uk

How long does planning permission last?

Full permission

Planning permission has always lasted for five years, with the requirement that reserved matters are submitted within three. This general time period has now been reduced. It is now the case that detailed planning permission, listed building consent and conservation area consent will normally be granted with the condition that the development or works must be begun within three years from the date on which the permission or consent was granted. Local planning authorities have the power to agree a longer or shorter duration where they consider it would be appropriate. There is little guidance to suggest under what circumstances that might be.

Outline permission

Where a local planning authority is considering an application for outline planning permission, it must grant it subject to conditions imposing two separate time limits. The first sets the time limit within which applications must be made for the approval of reserved matters. This will normally be three years from the grant of outline permission. The second sets the time limit within which the development itself must be started. This will usually be two years from the final approval of the last of the reserved matters. Local authorities have the power to vary these time limits as they see fit, which they may do in the case of major phased development proposals where a scheme may be implemented over many years.

What are planning conditions?

When you get planning permission it will be subject to planning conditions. This will include a time limit during which the project has to be started.

Conditions are extremely important and failure to comply with them can result in what is called a breach of condition notice (BCN) to which there is no right of appeal and which can be enforced through the courts by prosecution.

Conditions might be as simple as requiring that materials must match existing ones, or that all boundary treatments must be agreed. Some conditions have very expensive consequences. You need to be aware of the impact of conditions when negotiating on a planning application or if you're buying a building plot because they might seriously affect the value. For example, it would be usual for planning conditions to require the access to the plot to have clear lines of sight up and down the road so that it is safe. If these vision splays cross someone else's land, even by as little as a foot, then the permission cannot be implemented and the condition cannot be fulfilled without the neighbouring landowner's permission. This situation is called a ransom as the landowner simply holds you to ransom until you pay money in exchange for the right to fulfill the requirements of the condition. All ransom payments are settled by negotiation but the industry standard seems to be about a third of the development value of the site being transferred to the ransom holder. This is irrespective of the area of land involved. It is simply about unlocking the permission. Other conditions that can cause problems include drainage, archaeology and contaminated land. As always, 'caveat emptor' or buyer beware.

Conditions precedent are those that need to be cleared and formally agreed before the development starts. It must be negatively worded and unequivocal, using such a phrase as no development shall commence until... A condition which simply requires that something be done before the commencement of development is not a condition precedent in the legal sense. If you don't comply with a condition precedent, it's not a lawful start although such conditions may still be cleared and agreed retrospectively within the life of the permission. If they are not cleared within the three (or five) year lifespan of the permission, the development will be unlawful and unauthorised! This is particularly important when dealing with a potential site where a development was commenced with a view to keeping the permission alive in perpetuity. If the conditions precedent were not cleared when it was commenced, the permission will not be secured and the land may therefore have no development value. The relevant legal case is R (Hart Aggregates) v. Hartlepool DC ([2005] JPL 1603).

What happens if somebody objects to a proposal?

If the neighbours object don't panic. Just because someone objects does not mean that a planning application will necessarily be refused, and just because no one objects does not mean that permission will be granted. It is quite possible that a neighbour or the Parish or Town Council may not like what you wish to do, regardless of its acceptability in planning terms. (see Chapter 9 for more details).

Is planning just about conformity?

Unless a Planning Authority identifies specific characteristics of an area as being visually important, then just because something is different from its neighbours does not mean that it should necessarily be refused. You should not be afraid to be original and incorporate interesting and imaginative elements into the appearance of your home provided you can justify them in design terms. In a notable appeal decision many years ago, which permitted a glassfibre shark in the roof of a house in Headington, Oxford, the Inspector stated that it was not the purpose of planning to enforce a "boring and mediocre uniformity" on the built environment. If only there were more people in the planning world with that kind of attitude!

Oxford City Council first tried to get rid of the shark on the grounds that it was dangerous - but engineers pronounced the erection safe. The council then decided that the shark was a development under the Town and Country Planning Act, It was refused retrospective planning permission by Oxford City Council but the case was appealed and won!

Picture: Stephanie Jenkins

Chapter 3
THE RULES OF THE GAME

Planning decisions have to be based on a set of assumptions, which with a bit of luck go beyond the blind prejudice of local politicians. For this reason there are planning policies in place to help guide the location and form of new development. These are set out at both national and local level.

These planning policies comprise what are, in effect, the rules of this game. Just to ensure that things are as complicated as possible we currently have a system incorporating two different sets of rules and several sets of referees! We are currently operating under both the old rules – the system that has been in place since 1947 and which is now being phased out to be replaced by the Local Development Framework. In some areas there is a mixture of both and Wales and Scotland are evolving their own structures that are more akin to the old style development plan set up.

Because planning decision makers need to look at both planning policies and material considerations that might be relevant to a scheme before they make a decision, the analogy of weighing issues in the balance is often used. As a result, phrases such as significant weight, minimal weight or appropriate weight are employed to describe the importance given to the various factors that are taken into account by planning officers and planning committees.

Because the relative weight to be accorded to any factor is a matter for the decision maker, and a matter of interpretation, the process can be rather difficult to predict. It is always something of an educated guess as to what weight will be accorded to the different issues. This is why a clear understanding of which policies are relevant, where they are in the planning policy process and how well they accord with the most recent government advice is so important.

Government advice

Some of the most important material considerations that dictate what may be permitted are the latest pronouncements by central government on planning issues. Government policy advice comes in the form of planning circulars that often accompany specific pieces of legislation, planning policy guidance notes (PPG) that set out government policy, and more recently planning policy statements (PPS). The difference between PPG's and PPS's seems to be the degree of importance attached to them, the latter being more prescriptive and less flexible than the former. Rule by dictat might be putting it a bit strongly, or it might not. Of particular importance is the range of recent planning policy statements on Housing (PPS 3), the countryside (PPS 7) and others that are in the pipeline dealing with energy conservation and carbon emissions etc. For the residential developer, small builder and self builder PPS 3 is of vital importance in setting out the government's policy on where and when houses should be permitted and the issue of affordable housing provision. Where a local development plan is not up to date and when new government advice is issued, it is the government advice that takes precedence.

Development plans and the local development framework

The Development Plan System in the UK has been arranged in more or less the same way since 1947. This old style system, as it is often called, is being phased out in England and to a lesser extent in Wales, and will be replaced by the Local Development. This chapter sets out how both the 'old rules' and the local development framework system work.

When a planning authority considers whether or not to grant permission for a development the current starting point is:

Section 38(6) of the Planning & Compulsory Purchase Act 2004, which says "If regard is to be had to the development plan for the purpose of any determination to be made under the Planning Acts the determination must be made in accordance with the plan unless material considerations indicate otherwise".

The precise meaning of Material Consideration is difficult to define but generally most social, economic and environmental influences that have a bearing on the use of land are capable of being material to a planning decision. Most planning barristers are very hesitant to dismiss almost anything as a potential material consideration depending upon the circumstances. For example, the fact that people have objected to a development can be material but the weight to be accorded is largely dependent upon the substance of their concerns. However, the strength of feeling alone has, on occasion, been deemed material for example in the case of proposed new Bail Hostels.

The current system is one of transition between the old local plan approach and the new local development framework; much is obscured by the use of different jargon.

In effect, both arrangements involve the creation of planning policies to control and guide local development. These policies are given a degree of weight (ie importance) based upon the degree of public consultation and formal examination they have been subjected to and based on their conformity with current central government policy. So a recently formally adopted local development plan policy can be instantly reduced in importance upon the publication of new central government advice that contradicts it. Planning policy is an ever-changing set of goal posts that can alter during the processing of an individual planning application or more frequently during the processing of a lengthy planning appeal. During the current transition from old to new system, some local authorities have recently adopted old style plans that have significant weight and that have been 'saved' for the next three years. Others have

abandoned their old plans and a local policy vacuum exists while they try and sort out a new local development framework.

The 'old' rules

Under the now almost obsolete local plan system there are two kinds of arrangements, one involving county council administered structure plans plus the local plan and one in which they have been absorbed together into a single unitary development plan. The Scottish system retains this two-tier system at present.

Structure plan/local plan

The structure plan - dealing with county wide and strategic issues (produced by the county council)
The local plan - dealing with much more detailed and site specific issues (carried out by the district council or National Park Authority)
The minerals local plan (carried out by the county council)
The waste local plan (carried out by the county council)

Unitary authority planning

The unitary development plan (UDP) is a combination of a structure and local plan in one document.

In a unitary authority there is still the need for a waste local plan and a mineral local plan.

The two local plan and unitary plan systems aimed to set out the parameters of what should be allowed in any given area. Each plan was produced via several stages of public consultation followed by a local public inquiry. The local plan inspector would then submit a report to the secretary of state for ratification and the plan could then be modified and formally adopted. The process was intended to be a rolling programme that lasted about five years. In this system the local plan inspector's comments were not binding on the local authority.

The local development framework - faster & simpler?

Over the years there were criticisms of the old local plan system due to the time taken to produce local plans over a five-year rolling programme. With apparent good intentions and with typical evangelical reforming zeal, the government has complicated the system and introduced the new local development framework approach. It is intended to be a loose-leaf folder of documents that can, in theory, be updated more readily than the formally published local plan. The single formal local plan inquiry is now to be replaced by numerous less formal but equally time-consuming examinations in public associated with a greater level of public consultation than ever before. Anecdotal evidence consistently suggests that this new process is far more time-consuming, complex and numbingly bureaucratic than the previous one whilst at the same time allowing significantly less genuine local autonomy in decision-making.

In replacing the former combined structure and local plan approach, the Planning and Compulsory Purchase Act of 2004 introduced a new two-tiered plan system that dispenses with structure plans and comprises of:

■ Regional Spatial Strategies (RSS) – prepared by the regional planning bodies (or in London the spatial development strategy prepared by the Mayor of London). These set out a broad spatial planning strategy for how a region should look in 15 to 20 years time and possibly longer. These are intended to replace the previous regional planning guidance.

■ Local Development Frameworks (LDF) – a folder of local development documents prepared by district councils, unitary authorities or National Park authorities that outline the planning policies for the local area. These are intended to replace the previous local or unitary development plan.

Ironically this local development framework, together with the regional spatial strategy, is intended to be flexible and reactive while being forward looking and faster to prepare than the old local plan.

The new system appears to be evolving into a kind of series of small local plan making processes, rather than just the one.   Local authorities

are suffering severe staffing problems in attempting to cope with the significant additional work above and beyond the requirements of the old system.

Local Development Framework (LDF)

The contents of this folder of documents is not exactly the same in all areas but it generally contains:

- Development plan documents
- Local development scheme
- Statement of community involvement
- Annual monitoring report
- Supplementary planning documents
- (Occasionally) Local development orders and simplified planning zones

Local development framework documents may be classified as either legally required or optional. As you can imagine the optional documents will take a lower priority compared to the more pressing legally required ones. From a developer's point of view, it is the optional documents that appear most relevant and important in day-to-day practical terms, as they tend to deal with small-scale development control policies and potential future development sites.

Development plan documents (DPDs)

The local development framework must include a core strategy, site-specific allocations of land, a proposals map and may also contain additional optional development documents such as area action plans. These are classed as development plan documents (DPD) and outline the key development goals of the local development framework. All the documents must be consistent with each other and, of course, with the underpinning core strategy.

All development plan documents are subject to rigorous procedures of community involvement, consultation and independent examination which seem to be taking a great deal longer than was anticipated. They are also proving to be difficult to produce in tandem as changes to one may have a knock on effect on others so putting back their adoption and leading to requirements for additional consultations to deal with proposed changes.

Once they have been adopted, development control decisions should be based upon the development plan documents unless material considerations indicate otherwise. Development plan documents are also subject to a sustainability appraisal, a major and time consuming task in itself. All development plan documents have to be agreed by the Secretary of State so ultimately, notwithstanding all the local consultations, the real power has been further concentrated in central government.

Local development scheme

This is a required document. The local development scheme is the first step of the process and it sets out the 'project plan' for the production of the local development framework. Specifying which local development documents will be produced over the intended three-year period; when and in what order.

The local development scheme is subject to public consultation and acts as the starting point for interested individuals to get involved. Although it is a process driven part of the exercise, it is unlikely to be of practical interest to developers or even objectors other than in terms of indicating when their involvement is likely to be influential.

Local authorities submitted their local development schemes to the Secretary of State by the end of March 2005 and they are usually to be found on a local authority's website.

Statement of community involvement

This is a required document. The statement of community involvement

(SCI) has tended to be produced at the same time as the local development scheme as it underpins the process in explaining how and when planning authorities intend to consult local communities and other stakeholders through the production of each development plan document. This statement also specifies how local authorities will consult on individual planning applications.

The statement of community involvement encourages consultation at the earliest stages of each policy document's development so that local people are given an early opportunity to participate in plan making and, in theory, to make a difference. It seems likely that many communities will suffer from serious consultation fatigue after a short time as each document grinds its way through this process.

Every statement of community involvement must, to quote the government, 'Provide open access to information, actively encourage the contribution of ideas and representations from the community and provide regular and timely feedback on progress.' This will be no easy task given the number of development plan documents involved in each local development framework. Each development plan document becoming almost a mini local plan of the old type.

Core strategy

This is a required document. The core strategy underpins the whole thing and sets out the general policies and objectives to be delivered by the local development framework.

The core strategy is supposed to be closely liked to the delivery of the council's community strategy by setting out its spatial aspects and providing a 'long-term spatial vision'. The core strategy should express those parts of the community strategy that relate to the development and use of land and outline the council's hopes for delivering development. This includes the environment, reducing carbon emissions, leisure, housing and shopping etc. The community strategy can incorporate just about everything the council does - and many things it does not actually control but may have some involvement in - so it has the potential to be a vast, complex and hopelessly vague, exercise. Time will tell.

The core strategy must be kept up to date and all other development plan documents must be in conformity with it. It also has to conform to the relevant regional spatial strategy (or the spatial development strategy in London). It must also be in conformity with government advice and also be agreed by the secretary of state. Any change in any one of these variables can throw the whole thing out of line. Unlike the old system, the views of the government inspector are binding on the authority. Notwithstanding all the good intentions set out in the community strategy whether or not the policies are in place to help them happen will largely be in the hands of central government.

Site specific allocations

This is a required document and is a vital document for developers and local people. When this element was part of the previous simpler local plan process it tended to generate the most objections and representations to the plan and to the public inquiry. Now it is a separate document, it can only be done effectively once the core strategy is in place. Some core strategies hint at locations for development or even direct it specifically, so the process has been subdivided in a confusing and potentially misleading manner. The individual documents must comply with the core strategy, so if a site is mentioned then, on the face of it, it is a long way down the road to being allocated.

In theory, once a local development framework is completed, thereafter the site allocations local development frameworks will allow the local authorities to update allocations to reflect changes to other local development documents or implementation on the ground.

Promoting sites for development under the new rules

The chances of it getting a greenfield site developed for housing or anything else are extremely slim unless it is allocated for development in the local development framework. This system tends to have very long timescales with some local development framework documents seeking to make decisions about housing sites 10 years in advance. The problem is that if a site fails to be allocated in the first round of site specific allocation documents, it is not immediately apparent what happens next.

The local development framework was introduced with a fanfare of promises that it would be continually reviewed and revised and therefore be more flexible. The key to this promise of flexibility appears to be hidden in the Annual Monitoring Report that must be produced by local authorities to assess whether the policies are actually working. Part of this will, apparently, include an assessment of whether the housing delivery and site allocations are taking place as expected. In the probable event that national policy or regional spatial strategies require more housing than was initially forecast then opportunities will open up for new sites to be promoted and brought forward well before the anticipated 10 year plan period. In theory, if a site fails to be allocated initially there will be potential to push for its allocation every time the annual monitoring report indicates a chink in the local authority's armour, such as when they fail to deliver the housing anticipated by the local development framework. Recent guidance in PPS 3 emphasises housing delivery not just making plans and this may have real consequences for the ongoing promotion of sites, which are not successful in the first round.

Annual monitoring report

This document seems to be an unwelcome drain on the resources of local authorities due to the volume of work required to assess the progress and the effectiveness of a local development framework, particularly given the lengthy timescales at work in the development of land.

This annual monitoring report is intended to assess whether:

■ Policies are achieving their stated objectives and delivering sustainable forms of development

■ The original objectives behind the policies are still relevant
■ The housing targets set in the local development framework are being met

To achieve this goal, the annual monitoring report needs to include a complex range of local and standard (core output) indicators. It is self evident that an awful lot of work and hours will be devoted to this reporting mechanism at the expense of planning documents dealing with actual local planning issues. Although, due to the peculiarities of this new system, it may well be a key document for developers helping them to understand when new housing allocations will be required.

Proposals map

This is an important required document. The proposals map has to be adopted as a separate LDD and illustrates the site-specific allocations and other locational policies in map form. It will identify areas such as nationally protected landscapes like areas of outstanding natural beauty and green belt boundaries, local landscape designations such as areas of high landscape value, local nature reserves and conservation areas and areas of potential flood risk.

Separate inset maps may be used to show more detailed parts of town centres or particular area action plans. The adopted proposals map has the potential to be an ever-changing feature. If necessary it must be revised as each new development plan document is adopted so that it is up to date. Presumably each time it is changed, new public consultation requirements kick in which themselves take many months. The prospect of there ever being a fully adopted and up to date proposals map appears rather slim.

Area action plans

This is an optional development plan document. An area action plan (AAP) is a development plan document aimed at a specific location

or an area that has been identified as being in need of improvement, regeneration or protection.

The area action plan is intended to focus on proactive implementation and it may, therefore, involve more than just the actions of the local authority. It may seek to enable development for growth or regeneration purposes or to inhibit certain activities in the cause of nature conservation or historic interest.

Optional development plan documents

Different local authorities have created their own range of development plan documents dealing with the issues that concern them most in their area, much as the previous local plans used to do. They will normally include generic development control policies, all of which are very important for the day-to-day running of the developed control section of the planning department. It is the small-scale nitty-gritty of development control policies that affect the vast majority of applicants for planning permission for extensions, single dwellings and small schemes.

Supplementary planning documents

Optional supplementary planning documents (SPD) replace what were described as supplementary planning guidance, but they are the same animal. They add detail to policies laid out in development plan documents, or to a saved policy in an existing old style development plan. These may take the form of design guides, area development briefs, a master plan or issue-based documents.

Local authorities must consider the preparation of these as part of their statement of community involvement; they are also subject to a sustainability appraisal.

Supplementary planning documents are very definitely worth looking at, along with their previous incarnation, SPGs, as they often contain the nitty-gritty of design concerns and development related rules of thumb used by local authorities to assess the acceptability of development proposals

Local development orders/simplified planning zones

These are very definitely optional. Local authorities have the power to create local development orders and simplified planning zones where they want to relax planning controls for economic development and or environmental reasons.

A local development order extends permitted rights for certain forms of development.

A simplified planning zone is an area in which a local planning authority wishes to stimulate development and encourage investment. It operates by granting a specified planning permission in the zone without the need for a formal application or the payment of planning fees. A rare beast, normally used only where no one generally wants to invest, to try and encourage them to do so.

The use of carefully
matching materials
and detailing with the
correct proportions and
scale mean that this
extension effectively
remodels this house.

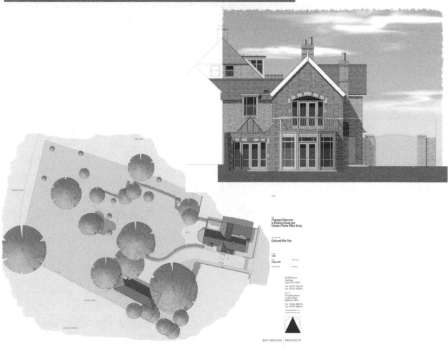

Chapter 4
EXTENSIONS

This chapter deals with the minor development proposals likely to be carried out by most homeowners at one time or another. What will be allowed tends to be a function of the combined influences of local plan policies; local supplementary planning guidance, permitted development rights, local politics and the knowledge and experience/reasonableness of the particular planning officer dealing with the application.

Do you need permission?

Most people who own a house will, at some stage, decide to improve it. And this often involves rubbing shoulders with the planners. It is a fairly ridiculous aspect of the current planning regime in the UK that if you apply for a single storey rear extension it is dealt with following more or less the same procedures as if you wanted to build a hundred houses. There are moves afoot to simplify applications or even eradicate the need for complex applications for simple proposals, but I will believe it when I see it.

If you want to extend your house, the first thing to establish is whether you need permission. If you understand the basics of permitted development rights (see Appendix 1) it should be fairly clear whether your plans will involve more than the allowed 15 per cent additional volume (or similar maximum number of square metres in Scotland) and whether what you want to build will exceed the normal four metre height limit. If you can possibly take advantage of permitted development, my advice is to do so.

Remember that when you have your planning permission for an extension, it is still possible to use your permitted development rights as long as you have finished all the permitted development-related building work before you start the scheme that actually has permission.

Once it is clear that you need permission to extend your house in the way you want, the first step is to think about how it will affect your neighbours; the second step is to think about the appearance.

This section is intended to help you decide whether what you want to do to your home is likely to receive planning permission. It should also be useful in suggesting other ideas and possibilities that you might not have considered. Most local authorities now produce supplementary design guidance aimed specifically at small-scale residential extensions. But remember that it is guidance and it should not be set in stone, each case must still be treated on its merits.

Planning – an art not a science

There are few hard or fast rules determining what will or won't receive planning permission. Exactly the same proposal may be perfectly acceptable in one location but be refused in another.

All planning authorities adopt slightly different policies and in different areas of the country certain aspects of a proposal may be considered more important than others. There will usually be a number of design solutions to any one planning problem and the good designer is worth their weight in gold. It is also a sad fact that the personality of the individual planning officer who deals with your application can have a profound influence upon your whole experience. Some planning officers are deeply negative and unhelpful whilst others are quite the opposite – it's the luck of the draw. You may be able to engage in pre-application discussions with the helpful planner in the hope that they will then deal with the resulting application, although that is not guaranteed.

A major investment

Some of the suggestions made in this chapter may result in an extension being more expensive to build. But consider:

■ However much you like a particular design and want to keep costs down, if it fails to get permission, it's worth nothing.

■ A cheaply built, badly designed addition may add little or no value to your property and could make it more difficult to sell.

In the case of a well-designed and carefully considered extension the reverse of the above is likely to be true. Any proposal is going to be a major investment of your money, so it is worth doing properly.

.

General principles

Householder planning applications are likely to be considered from two separate angles. The planner will be concerned about:

■ The effect of the proposal on the living environment of neighbouring properties.

■ The look of the proposal and the effect it will have on the appearance of the surrounding area, an essentially subjective judgement.

In making these judgements, the planner will apply a variety of general principles, which will probably appear in the supplementary planning guidance issued by a local authority. These are explained in this chapter and should be a useful guide as to what is likely to be acceptable. Before looking at these principles it is important to be aware of certain policy designations which could affect the overall level of control that may be imposed. These areas will be subject to specific planning policies that can be found in the relevant local plan, or local development framework for the area involved

Areas with special designations

If your house is located in an area, which has a special designation in planning policy terms, then the level of scrutiny of your proposal will be greatly increased. Such areas are:

■ Green belts
■ National Parks, Areas of Outstanding Natural Beauty and the Norfolk Broads
■ Conservation areas
■ Areas identified locally as of special character

I will consider each in turn.

Green belts

Areas of land around a large number of towns and cities are designated as green belt. The specific purpose of this designation is to prevent these towns and cities from expanding continually into the open countryside which surrounds them. The general policy applied to land within the green belt is to prevent, as far as possible, all new development. There are a limited number of exceptions to this policy, such as development required for agriculture.

Applications for house extensions in the open countryside or in villages within the green belt are likely to receive very careful consideration in terms of their visual and physical impact on the open and undeveloped character of their surroundings. The key jargon is 'Inappropriate Development', which is more or less anything that is not especially justified.

National parks, areas of outstanding natural beauty and the Norfolk Broads

These three designations are given in recognition of the special landscape qualities and natural beauty of these areas. In planning terms, such areas are considered highly sensitive to developments of any kind. So special scrutiny will be given to design, materials, visual prominence and the traditional local architecture will be valued. Permitted development rights are reduced and this is a reflection of the perceived importance of controlling inappropriate development.

Conservation areas

Local planning authorities will designate some areas of towns and villages as conservation areas. These are defined in the legislation as 'areas of special architectural interest, the character and appearance of which it is desirable to preserve or enhance'. The principle legal effects of designation are that most forms of building demolition require consent (conservation area consent), and that anyone proposing to fell or work on a tree must inform the local planning authority six weeks in advance. Failure to accord with either of these stipulations is an offence. Permitted development rights are also reduced. The consideration of all planning applications within conservation areas will be very thorough and excellent standards of design and materials will be demanded.

Emphasis will be given to the traditional styles, materials and design details found within the conservation area, although modern interpretations are a possibility if the council's conservation officer can be persuaded. But conservation does not mean preservation, some change is accepted and this designation is not a barrier to all new development. People who buy houses in conservation areas often seem to expect that all new development will automatically be refused. This is not the case.

Areas of special character

Many planning authorities have identified in their local plans parts of towns and villages which, though not special enough to warrant for conservation area status, have a special character that the Local Authority considers worthy of preservation. This designation may be given to all kinds of areas, from leafy suburbia to Victorian terraced houses. Find out what 'special character' has been identified and you will have a sporting chance of meeting the planners' requirements.

Other considerations:

Precedent

All planning applications are supposed to be considered individually and without prejudice. But planning authorities do attempt to be consistent and it would be unreasonable if two very similar proposals received very different decisions. This means that when a planning application is being considered, precedent will be an issue. But the best way to describe it is to require consistency in decision making when the planning context is materially similar.

Security

The design of an extension or position of a fence may affect the vulnerability of a house to burglary. This is a material consideration and the government has issued policies dealing with it. Although in a small-scale planning application security is unlikely to be a determining factor, you ought to bear it in mind for your own benefit.

Trees and shrubs

The quality and quantity of existing planting in a garden will have a crucial effect upon the potential appearance of any new extension or major alteration to a house. Try to keep as many existing trees and shrubs as possible when extending. The planners will wish to see them retained to maintain the setting of the house and street. They often attach conditions to ensure this and to ensure that additional trees are planted. Do bear in mind that if your proposals require the removal of a tree in your garden, or could affect its roots, then the local authority can decide to impose a Tree Preservation Order and this will probably kill your plans.

Overlooking

The more closely spaced houses are, the more important it is to consider privacy in the design of an extension. Privacy may be lost through the construction of an extension which allows views into the windows of a neighbouring property or into a nearby garden. Overlooking can also be caused by balconies, roof gardens or first floor conservatories.

Windows which cause an unacceptable degree of will not be permitted. In most cases this means that there should be no first floor windows on the sides of houses other than obscure glazed landing or bathroom windows. The key phrase to note here is 'unacceptable degree of overlooking'. This is because what is classified as 'overlooking' usually depends on window-to-boundary and window-to-window distances. Where windows currently overlook a neighbour, the addition of new windows on the same elevation is unlikely to be a problem.

Window to window distances

There is a generally acknowledged requirement of a minimum privacy distance of 21m between facing first floor windows. Ground floor windows are rarely a problem unless differences in ground levels cause them to be elevated above fence level. Extensions that would bring windows closer than this distance may not be acceptable. In situations where houses do not directly face one another then the minimum window-to-window distance may be reduced, because the problem of direct overlooking from one window to another may not occur.

Standards of what may be considered 'acceptable' levels of privacy are likely to be increased in locations where high levels of privacy are the norm and vice versa. For instance, in an area of secluded detached houses in large plots it may not be appropriate to allow an overlooking window on a neighbouring extension simply because the minimum 21m window-to-window distance is being complied with.

Window to boundary distances

The overlooking of the private areas of neighbouring rear gardens is undesirable and should be avoided. A first floor primary window will usually be considered to cause unacceptable overlooking if it is closer than ten and a half metres to the boundary of the neighbour's garden. This represents half the 21m window-to-window distance described above and is a minimum. When neighbouring gardens are currently entirely private then the local authority may try to ensure that windows in a new extension are positioned to avoid causing any overlooking at all and you can guarantee that the neighbours will object.

Overshadowing

Most people value very highly the amount of sunlight and daylight which comes through their windows. So it is important that extensions do not overshadow neighbouring windows or cause a serious loss of sunlight. However, as always it is a matter of the degree of overshadowing. Due to the movement of the sun, some windows are more or less likely to be overshadowed or to lose direct sunlight. Therefore, a rear extension may be permitted in one instance but not in another due to the orientation of the houses.

Planners do not normally measure these issues scientifically; they rely upon subjective judgement and rules of thumb set out in their Supplementary Planning Guidance (or Documents). However, a recent case touching the question of right to light poses some interesting questions as to the degree to which objectors to developments that have been considered acceptable in planning terms and actually granted permission may then be deemed unacceptable on the grounds of right to light in court and action then taken to demolish them. The relevant recent case is Court of Appeal in Regan v. Paul Properties DPF No.1 Ltd [2006].

The movement of the sun

If you are building a house or wish to extend one then it will help if you can acquire an accurate knowledge of the sun's movement during the day. You are then in a good position to judge what affect your development would have on neighbouring houses. Remember that just because a neighbour is happy with your ideas does not necessarily mean that the planner will be. It is their job, in theory, to protect the residential environment of houses in the public interest. Which sounds fine but makes no sense in cases where no one but the planner is bothered. The planner's assessment of overshadowing is likely to be quite subjective rather than scientific; it is based on a judgment about pleasant living conditions rather than quantifiable light levels, which also makes it a nonsense if the neighbours are happy. There has recently been some suggestion that changes could be made to the system that might take this on board but I doubt it will happen as local politicians and their planners naturally want to keep all the power they can.

The 45° Rule

A useful guideline, which is adopted by many planners, is the 45° rule. This is intended to prevent extensions having an overshadowing, dominating and overbearing effect on neighbouring properties. To comply with this rule, an extension should not extend beyond a line drawn at an angle of 45° from the nearest edge of the nearest window of the neighbouring house, excluding such things as bathroom, utility room or landing windows. For one or two storey extensions the line should be drawn from the nearest ground floor or first floor window.

Generally speaking, a stricter approach will be taken when dealing with two storey extensions than single storey ones because the potential for overshadowing is greater.

This 45° rule will not usually be applied rigidly, as many other factors can be involved. For instance, if the rear of a house already has very limited access to daylight or sunlight then even a neighbouring extension that meets the 45° rule can have an unacceptable effect. In some cases even small one or two storey extensions can cause serious overshadowing due to the design of neighbouring houses and the sun's position.

Oppressiveness

An extension or outbuilding may not overshadow or overlook, but it may have an oppressive and overbearing effect on a neighbour and create a poor aspect from their windows. This is difficult to quantify but if you think the visual effect would be to dominate the neighbouring house and garden then it is quite likely that the planners won't like it. This kind of issue is very subjective indeed and hard to argue against other than by comparison with other approved schemes or similar existing situations in the vicinity. A good designer also comes into their own in considering such issues at the outset.

Good design and the character of an area

There used to be a great deal of debate about how much planners should concern themselves in questions of good and bad design, now these phrases are embedded in both local and national policies, without any common ground as to what they mean in practice. There is a fine line between personal opinions about what is and what is not attractive. Few professional judgments about these things are genuinely free from personal opinion. There is general agreement that planners should not concern themselves with matters of personal preference but distinguishing preference from cold judgment can be fiendishly difficult and it can make predicting the outcome of an application almost impossible.

To understand the approach taken by most planners, it is useful to consider poor design simply as a lack of design. Where there has clearly been no thought put into the appearance of a proposal and no attempt has been made to respect the character of an existing building or its surroundings, then this can fairly be described by the planners as bad design. The design and access statements that are now required are, in many cases, pointless. However, they can be useful in some cases allowing developers to explain and justify why certain approaches have been taken and this, therefore, requires planning officers to deal with design issues in a similar rigorous fashion.

Planning does not mean that just because something is different, then it is undesirable and should be refused. Planners can identify when a house or its surroundings has no special character or features that can be identified as being of particular value or worthy of preservation. In practice, there is more freedom of design than a lot of planning committees and some planning officers would like to admit.

Front-facing extensions

There is considerable scope on many houses for a front extension of moderate or small size. Extending the front of a house may be useful in providing a larger lounge, large porch, downstairs WC or even additional bedrooms. However, the front of the house is likely to be visually the most sensitive and prominent part and changes to it need to be considered carefully and be capable of justification in architectural terms.

The building line

Conformity with the building line in a street becomes more important the more rigidly it has been complied with in the past. This means that in areas where all the houses are a similar distance to the road, then building in front of this line would be very apparent and change the appearance of the area. In less regimented areas where many houses have different relationships with each other and are set at different distances from the road, or have substantial front gardens, then there is likely to be more flexibility and potential to build forward of the existing building line.

The design of some houses will enable quite large and substantial front extensions, particularly where a house is designed in an L-shape. Filling in the 'L' is often quite acceptable because the extension will come no closer to the road than the existing house and neighbours are unlikely to be affected.

The character of the area

Filling in gaps between houses can have a radical effect on the appearance of a street. Many planning authorities adopt the rule that no two-storey extensions should come within one metre of a shared boundary. A larger gap is likely to be required on the edge of towns or in rural areas where it is necessary to maintain greater space between buildings in order to preserve the spacious character of an area. The best guide to the size of side extension that would be permitted is to consider the general layout of houses in the road. Single storey side extensions are not usually considered a problem in this respect because the gap between houses will still be apparent. When considering the potential for infill plots, bear in mind that the increased need to allow higher densities is resulting in developments that are actually very different from the character of existing areas. The now superseded PPG3 policy requirements for high minimum densities have required planners to accept developments that are radically out of keeping with the character of the area. This pressure has now been reduced slightly in the recently issued PPS 3, which recognises the need for family-sized houses with gardens. It is sometimes difficult to identify consistency in the approach taken within single authorities to this contentious issue of housing density.

Terracing effect

The terracing effect is a phrase used to denote the effect of infilling gaps between previously semi-detached or detached houses, producing what appears to be a continually built-up frontage. It tends to be very unpopular with people who feel that their houses are devalued because of the actions of neighbours, although such devaluation is not a planning matter. Building bedrooms above garages is a popular form of extension on modem estates where the design often lends itself to this type of change.

An alternative approach to extending is to leave the existing house untouched and add the extra space in a distinct and clearly new addition. The extension to this thatched cottage leaves theoutline of the original building clearly visible.

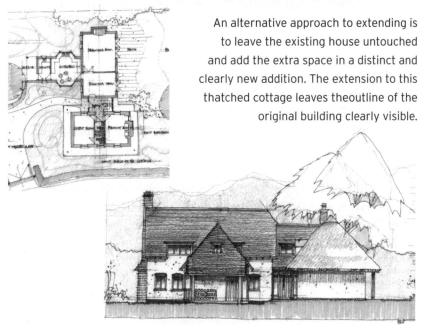

Joining the old with the new

When building an extension the best means of providing a clean join between the old and the new is to ensure that the extension is slightly set back just forward of the wall to which it is adjoined. The alternative is to use the extension to remodel the entire house in an attractive way resulting in a different design of property.

If the house is not being remodeled as a whole, there are two major benefits of setting back the new extension:

■ It is practically impossible to get an exact match between old and new bricks or other materials. Setting back avoids a scruffy and mismatched join and creates a neat appearance regardless of the precise match of materials.

■ Setting back helps to ensure that the original building keeps its essential character and design after the extension has been added. For example, a matched pair of semi-detached houses can sometimes be spoilt in appearance if a large extension to one is allowed to unbalance the pair but a set back enables one to recognise the position of the original semi.

Roof height and shape on side extensions

In general a roof height lower than the original is desirable – it should normally be no higher. Any setting back on the front elevations should be carried through to the roof level. All two-storey side extensions should have roofs of the same pitch as the original house, and have tiles or slates as near a match as possible to the original. Flat roofs will generally be frowned upon, and particularly those which are visible from a public area. Flat roofed extensions above single storey are unlikely to be approved today.

Sometimes areas are characterised by the existence of flat roofed garages. In this kind of situation the planners would be unjustified in insisting on pitched roofs on new single storey side extensions. Although sometimes cheaper to build, flat roofs often cost the same as pitched roofs and the latter usually need far less future maintenance. In the circumstances where a flat roofed side extension is the only option, a false pitch to the front can be an acceptable compromise.

If you are considering building over an existing garage, check that the foundations are adequate to cope with the additional load before going to the expense of making a planning application.

Rear extensions:

Two-storey rear extensions

Potential harm caused by overlooking or overshadowing will need to be considered carefully. Irrespective of those problems, some planning authorities seek to impose an arbitrary maximum of three metres in depth on rear extensions. In the case of terraced houses or small semi-detached houses this may be reasonable but otherwise such a restriction could be unjustified, particularly on a detached house with a large plot. In such a case it could be worthwhile appealing against a refusal unless clear justification is provided by the planning authority in terms of unacceptable design or harmful effects on the residential environment of neighbouring houses.

Roof height & shape on two storey rear extensions

As with other forms of extension, it is recommended that roof pitches should match the rest of the house and that the roof height should be set lower than the main ridge. Flat roofs are normally an eyesore and are best avoided.

The height of a pitched roof can be reduced by the use of dormer windows or skylights which enable the roof space itself to be utilised. Using a hipped, twin gable or valley roof may also reduce the height and physical bulk of a roof. Where the roof threatens to block out the sun, sloping it away from the affected neighbour can help to reduce the overshadowing effect. A part single-storey, part two-storey extension can often make the most of a restricted site.

Single-storey rear extensions

Most houses are able to accommodate and benefit from some form of single-storey rear extension. Provided that the materials used are suitable and the roof pitch is in keeping, then the possibility of a harmful impact on the appearance of the house is likely to be limited. Flat roofs, should be avoided.

Overshadowing and overlooking are obviously less likely to be a problem than with a two-storey extension. However, the proximity of neighbouring windows and the movement of the sun will still need to be considered. Overlooking could be a problem if a roof top patio were created or if there are different ground levels between neighbouring properties.

As a general rule, it is helpful not to build directly on the boundary and to keep the roof height low so that any effect on neighbours is minimised.

Garden areas

Some planning authorities still have standards for desirable minimum private garden areas or minimum garden depths in order to resist the overdevelopment of residential areas. However, such standards are becoming harder to justify in the face of increased pressure to permit high-density developments and to take full advantage of previously developed sites in urban locations. Such garden area policies are usually flexible but they need to be considered if you are proposing to extend and have only a small rear garden. The minimum depth of rear garden required is usually 10.5 metres.

Loft conversions

Many houses and bungalows offer enormous potential for the conversion of roof space into additional rooms. Roof conversions can take many forms: utilising roof lights, dormer windows or even involving the creation of a complete new storey on top of an existing house. Remember that internal conversions normally do not require planning permission and roof extensions for dormer windows can often be done as permitted development.

The most successful roof conversions in planning terms are generally those that have the least visual impact. The most useful roof conversions in practical terms are those that create the most amount of internal space. This conflict requires compromise; any dormer windows should be physically small in proportion to the size of the roof as a whole. If they are very large and bulky they will detract from the character of a house and may not get permission. As a guide, the size of the dormer should represent less than half the distance between the ridge and eves of the main roof.

On many modern houses the size of the roof space will not allow a useable conversion into bedrooms without the addition of more space than a traditional dormer can provide. Large flat roofed dormers can be acceptable if they are constructed on the rear (or least public) elevation and do not make the house look top heavy. Although, as always, if an area is characterised by flat roofed front facing dormers then it is likely that further dormers would be approved.

Converting a bungalow into a house

There are many bungalows that can satisfactorily be converted into two-storey dwellings by the use of dormer windows or rooflights. Some bungalows however do not have adequate roof space to allow this. Sometimes it is possible to convert a bungalow into a house by increasing the height of the roof in its entirety. It may then be necessary for dormers to be used, or it may involve the creation of a full additional storey. The economics of this approach are normally highly questionable. Everyone I have ever met who has undertaken such a project seems to wish that they had knocked it down and started again. Refurb build costs are often higher than newbuild.

One thing that needs to be established above and beyond the questions of detail and specific design issues is: 'will there be an objection to the conversion of a bungalow into a house?' The answer to this question depends very much upon the character of the surrounding area and the physical relationship between the existing bungalow and its neighbours.

Extensions to houses in open countryside

Many of the factors that restrict the size of possible extensions to houses in towns and villages do not apply to houses situated in open countryside. Such houses may have few, if any, immediate neighbours. Problems of overlooking and overshadowing will therefore not apply and there may be no clearly identifiable 'character of the area' with which to come into conflict.

This does not necessarily mean, however, that the maximum size of an extension will depend simply upon the amount of land available. In areas of countryside that have special designations and, to a lesser degree, in open countryside as a whole, national and local planning policies tend to emphasise a restrictive approach to new development. The purpose of this is, in theory, to protect the attractive appearance of rural areas. The reality is that people who have bought into the rural dream do not want anything to change; they want to protect their investments and will routinely oppose all new developments as a matter of course. The planning policies reflect this. As a consequence, in many areas it is not as easy to get planning permission to turn small cottages into larger houses as it once was.

Unless the local planning authority indicate otherwise, it would be reasonable to expect to have to restrict extensions so that they remain in proportion with the existing house. Extensions that enlarge a house by in excess of 50 per cent may be frowned upon, particularly in sensitive and prominent locations. Increasing numbers of local authorities actually include percentage limits within their policies to try and keep a lid on the enlargement of houses in rural areas.

Outbuildings and garages

Be sure to check out the possibilities available under permitted development as the local authority are unlikely to let you know, even if they see you struggle to get permission for something that with a few minor changes would not need permission at all.

If you need to apply for permission for outbuildings or a detached garage, then considerations of design will be as relevant as for other householder proposals. The design of free-standing garages should relate to that of the house and be built of similar (or complementary) materials.

When the design of the house and its location is mundane, then a more standard style of garage may be acceptable. Clearly the match of materials and design will not be as important to the appearance of a house as in the case of a physically linked extension.

The siting of garages is important to the appearance of a street. The space needed for a garage with an area for turning and additional parking will be considerable. A minimum distance of five and a half metres between garage doors and the highway will normally be required when a garage faces the road. As a consequence most garages are located or accessed down one side of the house. However, where there are garages situated forward of the house in a road, and front gardens are large, a garage in the front garden need not be impossible. In this case the amount of screening and planting available can have a significant effect on the look of the proposal.

Materials and attention to detail

The quality and choice of materials will be vital in achieving an attractive end result. There will normally be a condition attached to the planning permission, which states that materials must match the existing materials to the satisfaction of the planning authority. It is always advisable to submit a sample of the materials to be used to the planning department and to gain written confirmation that they are acceptable – that way you are fully covered in the event of a dispute in the future.

The detailed features of a building are just as important as the overall scale and design. It will improve the appearance of any extension enormously if the detailed design reflects the details on the existing house. For instance where a particular brick bonding is used it should be copied. In older buildings decorative brickwork was often used and other features such as interesting barge boards or chimneys may exist. If there are such features they should be echoed in the extension to help improve its appearance and integrate the new with the old.

The proportions and styles of doors and windows should match the existing house. This will be particularly important if the house is an older style building with some character. If an older style house (Victorian or earlier) has had original attractive sash windows removed, it may be a great opportunity to reinstate modern equivalents, which can look very similar. In my opinion aluminum or UPVC windows will always spoil the look of an old house.

Parking and access

Planning authorities will consult the local highway authority regarding the effect of planning applications on parking provision and road safety. As a general rule all new houses, and houses which are extended, will be required to have adequate on site parking spaces. The actual standards will differ throughout the country and be dependant to some extent upon the location and character of an area. In very urban locations they will accept lower parking provision based on the dubious logic that public transport will be available so residents will not need a car. True in some cases and in London, no doubt, but in most owner-occupied developments one car per adult is realistic.

Usually houses with up to three bedrooms will need to have a minimum of two parking spaces. In some areas where on street parking is becoming a problem (such as tightly developed modern estates) additional spaces will be required for each bedroom added by way of an extension. This is based on the simple logic that the bigger the house the more potential there is for car ownership and traffic generation. Such standards follow research into traffic movements generated from houses and estates. In competition with this common sense approach is government pressure to impose maximum parking availability, not minimum provision. All based on the notion that fewer spaces will pressurize people to use other modes of travel such as public transport. Many local planning authorities

4

are learning from bitter experience that this is a flawed strategy as high density estates with inadequate parking become overrun with cars.

The loss of substantial areas of front garden to provide parking spaces is likely to be frowned on by planners. This is despite the fact that you may turn your entire front garden into a hard standing without planning permission. However, remember that it is in the best interests of the appearance of the house and the street to retain as much greenery as possible.

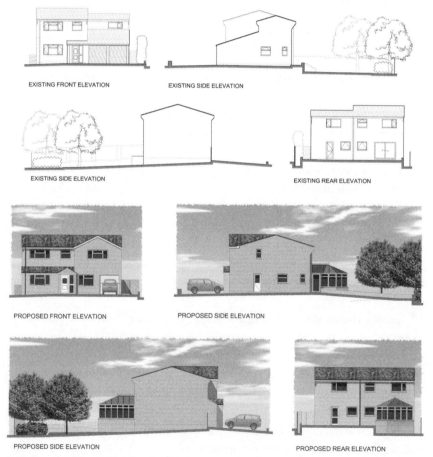

EXISTING FRONT ELEVATION

EXISTING SIDE ELEVATION

EXISTING SIDE ELEVATION

EXISTING REAR ELEVATION

PROPOSED FRONT ELEVATION

PROPOSED SIDE ELEVATION

PROPOSED SIDE ELEVATION

PROPOSED REAR ELEVATION

This house was no architectural jewel when built, but efforts to enlarge it still needed careful thought. The presentation drawings are invaluable in making the best of what is a significant and successful enlargement.

Extensions & minor developments planning checklist

1. Will the extension create overlooking or loss of privacy to neighbours?

2. Is there loss of sunlight or overshadowing of neighbouring windows or patio?

3. Is there a danger of the terrace effect or a dominating effect on neighbouring property?

4. Do the roof pitches on dormers or extension match the existing house?

5. Are the roof heights of extensions lower than the existing house?

6. Is a set-back in the walls and roof necessary to create a visual break or ensure decent match between old and new?

7. Does the extension fill a visually important space in the street scene or layout of an estate?

8. Are adequate parking spaces retained within the boundaries of the house?

9. Is there a reasonable amount of rear garden area remaining?

10. Do the detailed features on the extension match the existing house?

11. Are any trees affected or to be planted?

12. Is there an issue or foul or surface water drainage to be considered?

13. Is there any flooding or a watercourse nearby that might result in a flood risk assessment being needed.

14. Is the site contaminated?

15. Are the ground conditions likely to lead to expensive foundations?

16. Are there any covenants or easements on the deeds that could affect the development?

17. Are there any routes of services such as sewers or drains that could cause development problems?

18. Are there any rights of way, private or public, that cross the site, has the solicitor confirmed this?

19. Do you know the planning circumstances of surrounding land? Are their planning permissions that could be implemented or currently under consideration?

20. Are you absolutely positive that you need planning permission or could you actually be happy with slightly less and build it under permitted development?

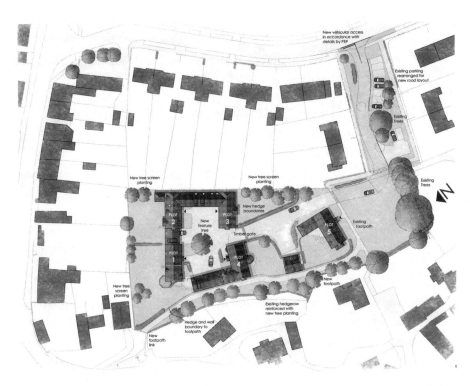

That illusive prize (above), a potential development site clearly within a built up area. But objections from neighbours are of course guaranteed. While small infill plots (below) are becoming harder to find and may perhaps on the endangered list if the proposed planning gain tax removes the incentive for people to sell off their surplus garden land. Below left shows the plot in relation to the area and below right the existing and proposed houses.

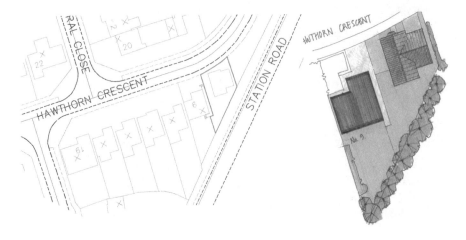

Chapter 5

PLANNING FOR NEWBUILD

Residential development & building plots

The starting point for any prospective developer, large or small, is very simple; it's finding the land to build on. Not the design of the house or the perfect location but just finding a building plot, almost any building plot, is the biggest challenge. But land only becomes a building plot when it's got planning permission. As I mentioned in the introduction to this book, planning permission transforms the value of a site. For example, an agricultural acre is worth about £3000 but the same acre with permission for residential development could be worth £2 million. So planning may be a hassle involving risk, delays and possible disappointment but it is also the best opportunity available to make money and/or build the house you want. Many of the design considerations mentioned in the chapter on extensions will be relevant to the detailed elements of any new build scheme.

Finding the land

It is quite possible to buy a building plot that already has planning permission as many are currently for sale on the open market. But the market is not quite as open as it appears and the most valuable and most desirable plots rarely get beyond the estate agent's door. Most local agents are very friendly with local builders and developers and because building land is scarce the use of introduction fees and further property re-sale fees ensures that estate agents

5

tend to place building land with people they already know in the development industry. Land for sale on the genuinely open market is likely to be overpriced or have some problem associated with it. And the planning permission may not itself be all that it seems. An outline consent only establishes the principle of building a house; there may be no detail at all about the size of the house or where on the plot it must be built . So if you buy a building plot with only outline permission you may find yourself involved in an uphill struggle to build a decent sized house or be limited to where on that plot you can build. There are plenty of outline planning permissions around, which offer far less development potential than the size or location of the plot would at first suggest. A detailed permission (also called full permission) will include all the aspects of the sighting, access, design and appearance of the permitted house, so there is much more certainty about what you are getting for your money.

If you do come upon building land in the right location with the benefit of planning permission but the nature of the approved scheme doesn't quite suit you, it may well still be worth buying. There are many different ways of developing any one site. Just because permission exists for, say, five bungalows, that doesn't mean you will necessarily have to build bungalows. Equally, house types can be made larger and sometimes permission for more houses can be achieved, which of course is where the real money is made.

The alternative to buying land that already has permission is to identify land yourself and to create your own building opportunities. This is where you can win, by either improving an existing planning permission or by adding value to land that hasn't been spotted as having development potential. There are a large number of potential building sites scattered throughout most towns and villages in the country; it is difficult not to see a potential building plot when looking at any Ordnance Survey plan or aerial photograph. It is vital to be able to quickly distinguish between sites with potential and those that are hopeless.

Greenfield sites

There's no point in attempting to get planning permission on virgin agricultural land unless it has been specifically allocated for development through the local plan or identified within the relevant local development framework

(LDF) for the area concerned. Prior to the publication of the government's Planning Policy Guidance Note 3 (PPG3), now superseded by Planning Policy Statement 3 (PPS 3), it was possible to make a successful planning application for development on a green-field site. This could be done as a rounding off proposal or as development within or on the edge of a settlement, whether or not the land was actually within a defined settlement boundary. But PPG 3 effectively killed this opportunity and instead made the high-density development of 'previously developed' land an overriding priority. For this reason, the possibility of getting planning permission on a field is, for the time being a non-starter. Meanwhile towns and villages are the focus of small and medium-sized developers' attention.

Previously developed land

Known colloquially as brownfield land this includes private gardens, industrial sites, commercial land, in fact just about any land containing non-agricultural buildings. There has been an explosion of intensive residential development on all kinds of commercial and industrial land and within the gardens of large houses in our cities, towns and villages. Competition for previously developed land is very intense. It nonetheless represents the best opportunity for new build development. For a single dwelling a straightforward infill plot in a back garden represents the ideal but there are plenty of knockdown and replacement opportunities. The classic small bungalow in a large plot still exists and can still be bought with patience and persistence.

Option agreements and conditional contracts

The great news is that you do not need to own land to make a planning application on it. It is quite possible to make an application on someone else's property and reap the benefits. There is a slight catch as the planning permission goes with the land not with the person who applies for it so you need to have done a deal with the owner before you start. It is quite usual for developers and speculators to use what's called an option agreement that secures their right to buy a piece of land if and when they get planning permission. If they don't get the permission they don't buy the land. The alternative legal mechanism is to

5

exchange contracts on the purchase of a site and make completion dependent on the receipt of satisfactory planning permission. Individuals and companies can use either of these two approaches to buy building land without taking unacceptably large financial risks.

Local authorities currently charge £265 to submit a planning application for a single house and let's say the professional fees cost about £3000. Your total speculation on a single plot could be less than £4000, which if it brings you a building opportunity at a good price is a risk worth taking. You need to be aware that the competition for finding building land is intense; there are people who spend every day of their working lives trawling through ordnance survey plans and aerial photographs looking for development opportunities.

As an individual or small builder you can still be successful in competing with these people but you need to know what your particular advantages are compared to the full-time professional land finders. Your major advantage, as an individual and a local, is the network of contacts and people you know in a local area who can give you leads to potential building plots. Coupled with this, you're likely to have knowledge of a particular neighbourhood and can therefore spot development opportunities on the ground.

Professional advice

My experience over almost 20 years, both as a local government planning officer and as a consultant, has shown me that there are two ways of using professional advice. The first is to delegate almost the entire activity to planning professionals; the second is to use such advice selectively, get involved yourself and take advantage of your local knowledge of a particular area.

For a self-builder or small business with a limited budget, throwing money at the problem of finding and getting planning on a plot is not wise. It's far better to focus on where you want to build and work closely with your professional advisors to maximise the chances of success. Planning is all about context, what may be acceptable on one side of the street could well be refused on the other. What is acceptable in one local authority could be totally impossible in another. The rules of the planning game are not clear-cut. They are expressed as development plan policies produced by local authorities to guide where new housing or commercial development is to be located and what kind of developments should be built in their particular area.

Planning policies

The development plan policies are a mixture of fairly clear site-specific allocations and development boundaries and a range of highly subjective criteria for what will and won't be acceptable in various contexts. The simplest polices will include lists of villages where they may accept new houses being built with a list of qualifying criteria. Villages and towns normally have a development boundary, or settlement boundary within which the principle of new development is allowed. Outside the development boundary, land will normally be classified as countryside where very restrictive planning policies are in place. The more subjective policies talk about development 'fitting in with the character and appearance of the area' and 'not causing harm to the amenities of the locality', which in plain English just means the planners have to like it. Trying to comply with these subjectively worded policies is very difficult without the help of an experienced designer or planning consultant who can interpret what they mean, often by what they don't say.

Looking at the local plan is still worthwhile and can enable you to discount areas from your search for land. In addition to these local plan policies there are special designations, which affect whole swathes of the country and that will have an influence on whether you can get permission to build a house. Designations like an area of outstanding natural beauty, national park, green belt and conservation area are very important but have different implications. Green belt is probably the strongest designation and it is often misunderstood, most areas of the countryside are not green belt. It is a planning status that only affects clearly defined areas of land around some of the major towns and cities. The issue of development plan policies is dealt with more fully in Chapter 3.

Site-specific issues

Once you have an understanding of the planning context of a location in terms of the policies and designations it is worth thinking about the site-specific issues related to your particular plot of land. If you are considering building on the large gardens of existing houses within the built-up area of a large town or village the issues will revolve around the direct impact on the character and appearance of the area and on the neighbours.

Before getting too excited about the development potential, check out the planning history to make sure it hasn't previously been attempted and refused. If it is a site with no adverse planning history make sure there are no particular local planning policy issues. An example is in a conservation area where retaining the gardens may be considered important. Assuming there are no obvious policy concerns you need to check that there are no trees subject to a Tree Preservation Order that could prevent development from happening. It's also vital to check whether the site falls within one of the Environment Agency floodplain maps that will result in the need for a flood risk assessment.

If the principle of building houses still appears sound then think about the details; can you build houses where they will not overshadow the neighbours? Can you design them so windows will not cause overlooking? Is there safe access onto the road with good visibility in each direction? Many potential plots are blighted by having substandard access. You may need to employ a professional highway consultant or planning consultant who can confirm that the access does meet the visibility requirements of the local authority.

Local politics

Planning can get very political, neighbours and parish councils often object for no other reason than they do not like change. Neighbours can become a thorn in your side and gather together all sorts of petitions and letter writing conspiracies among the other neighbours just to try and stop any development of any kind. The great fear is property devaluation and this is coupled with a blend of sour grapes, envy and general suspicion. This evil cocktail is then fed to the local ward councillor who is duty bound to represent the views of their electorate. If the application then goes to the planning committee, local hostility can drive the councillors to delay or even refuse proposals that are actually perfectly acceptable in planning. There is a danger in overreacting to every little objection once you have made the application but at the same time you should do everything possible to sweet talk the potential opposition. If this means modifying the scheme to pacify them it could be worth doing.

Planning officers

People who are successful at getting planning permission know how to play the game in the local area. There are loopholes and tactics that can maximise the chances of winning. It's important to understand that the planning officers don't get into trouble for saying no, they get into trouble by being too enthusiastic and too positive. Most planning managers see their job as development prevention in accordance with the local politicians' general stance. This means that negotiating and making them feel important is a useful approach.

Because planning officers feel the need to meddle with more or less anything you submit, it's a good idea to either apply for a very modest scheme that they will have trouble criticising or to apply for more than you want and then negotiate downwards. My recommendation is generally to go in small just to get the planning permission. Once you have planning permission for a modest, perhaps commercially unviable scheme, you can then make an application for a bigger, better, more viable alternative.

Planning departments are under great pressure to deal with applications within eight weeks of submission so they normally will not negotiate on a current application. Be prepared to withdraw a proposal if necessary so you can negotiate your way to an approval. It's a real danger to hang out for absolutely everything you want if this results in refusal because you may then be forced to appeal which is a real lottery. Once the appeal inspector has made a pronouncement it can be very damaging to the long-term prospects of a site.

Permitted development rights and new homes

Permitted development covers all the things that you can build that don't need planning permission. Your average house can be extended by 15 per cent

5

of its volume (and a similar size in square metres in Scotland) under permitted development, although this is a once only allowance. It's also possible to insert roof lights, carry out loft conversions, put in new window openings, build porches and install new external doors under permitted development.

If you're replacing an existing house with another, watch out for a condition of the new planning permission that takes away permitted development rights. This condition only comes into force when you actually start the new house so the trick is to take advantage of the permitted development rights related to the existing property before you start the new permission.   Permitted development is considered more fully in Appendix 1

Presentation

Being able to present your scheme effectively and attractively is important because planning authorities grant permission for what is really only a picture. The nicer the picture the more likely you are to get permission. So money spent on drawings and photo-simulated images of your development could be well worth spending.

Computer generated images (CGI) may be relatively expensive, but they are an excellent way of showing planners what the finished development will look like and can certainly help increase your chance of success. The finished development (right) looks remarkably like the CGI image (left) where the sun always shines!

Single plot replacement dwellings

Building plots for single dwellings with planning permission are difficult to get your hands on. If you can find one at an affordable price in the right location you will not be the only one who has spotted it. There will probably be a race to buy it in competition with other self-builders and local developers and it may finally be sold to the estate agents best mate – a local builder. Faced with these difficulties some people take extreme measures and gamble serious amounts of money on sites that don't have planning permission. Sometimes this works but more often than not people lose out big-time. If you are seeking a single plot the best and most realistic alternative is to buy a house for its land. In planning jargon you get a building plot by getting permission for a 'replacement dwelling'. This approach has many advantages over a virgin plot in addition to the fact that it is a realistic option for the self-builder.

House valuations and land value

Replacement dwelling opportunities are not always obvious and people are instinctively reluctant to think about demolishing a perfectly good house. This includes estate agents, so the value of property is usually based on the type of house and its size and condition, rather than looking at the land itself as a potential source of additional value. If you are fairly ruthless and look at property details in terms of the cost per square metre of land, it can become pretty clear that, due to the massively high price of building plots in desirable locations, the prospect of demolishing an existing small house and replacing it with a bigger one can be cost-effective. And don't assume this only works with replacing a small bungalow. There are potential plots on which to build £1m-plus homes in the South East where the existing four bed property may sell for a figure in excess of £500,000. Spend a further £300,000 on a luxury replacement and you are still significantly in profit.

Risk

Most self-builders and small developers are not speculators but just want to build houses. This means that avoiding risk is important and buying an existing house with a view to demolishing it is very much like buying a building plot with a planning permission that you then intend to change. The principle of a dwelling is established and provided you haven't paid above market value,

5

your investment should be secure. But in the same way as looking at a plot with outline planning permission, you need to have a full appreciation of what the likely planning policy restrictions will be on the size of house you can build.

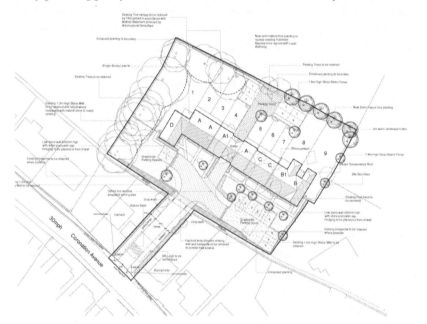

Ian Sullivan Architectural Design Ltd, Swindon. 01793 612663

Once an anathema in planning terms, back land developments are now often the only practical way to squeeze more houses into urban areas in accordance with government policies. The question should be asked as to whether it is not more harmful using up remaining green areas in built-up locations than building on some of the 90 per cent of undeveloped land located outside these areas.

Replacement dwelling policies

Replacing a small bungalow with a six bed three-storey detached house is a realistic proposition in some locations and a total impossibility in others. It depends upon the wording of the relevant planning policies in the local development plan (or local development framework). Specifically in the open countryside and areas designated as green belt, planning authorities often have in place policy restrictions on the increase in size of dwellings that will be permitted. The purpose of these policies is to keep a lid on the allowed amount of new development in an area but the subplot is that of social engineering. In many planning authorities, there is an unrealistic belief that small houses

5

in beautiful locations will be affordable housing for local people. The irony is that the reverse is, of course, true as restrictive planning policies create scarcity and drive prices upwards. So, when it comes to replacing the small bungalow with a large house to take advantage of a beautiful view just be sure that the planning constraints will enable you to add a reasonable amount of floor space to make the project worthwhile.

The relevant policies will usually be available on the council's own website – but this isn't the whole story and there are often loopholes which can be exploited. Ask for written copies of all relevant policies as older, more helpful ones may still be in place and may still adopted but not listed on the web.

Site specific issues

Having established that it makes sense to buy this property solely for its land value and that the general planning policy context is favourable to build a decent sized house, you need to check out the site itself. This means understanding what physical constraints, legal limitations and detailed planning influences will need to be taken into account in the design and positioning of your new house.

Special local designations

Look at the planning situation methodically and check out what planning permissions or refusals exist on the site in case someone has already had problems that you should avoid. Find out if the site is in a specially designated location. For instance:

■ Area of Outstanding Natural Beauty, which prioritises landscape impact
■ Conservation Area, where new development must 'preserve or enhance' the character and appearance of an area
■ The setting of nearby listed buildings where you need to demonstrate that what you want to build doesn't harm their historic setting
■ Floodplain – check that the site is not within an area liable to flood or close to a watercourse that could give rise to drainage problems or objections to increasing in the size of footprint of the house.

Impact on neighbours

Think about issues of privacy and the potential for your new property to overlook neighbours in a way that could create objections and planning problems and vice versa. Are there neighbouring windows that actually overlook this site in a way that restricts where you would want to build the new house? Confirm that the Highways engineers are happy for you to change the access arrangements and make sure it is physically possible in terms of visibility splays, highway safety and space for parking and turning. You may want to build a double garage but check that this does not impact on neighbours or block sight lines.

Site layout

Having understood the nature of the site and its limitations you will then need to employ an architect/designer to come up with a replacement dwelling that suits both the site and your requirements within your budget. The relevant planning department will probably have published supplementary guidance about the design of new houses in their area and they might expect you to produce a design statement justifying what you want to build. If you sketch out the different legal, planning and physical constraints and access points on a site-plan, this will often dictate both the size and position of the new house, so creating a basic site layout. Using this as a starting point you will at least know that what you're intending to build is physically possible and avoids any legal problems and doesn't generate any obvious conflict with neighbouring properties in planning terms.

House design

Choosing the design of your new house is very tricky because it's so subjective. Many self-builders in particular fall in love with a style of house and then try and find a plot upon which to build it. This is rarely possible because it is the plot itself that tends to dictate the style of house. So where do you start in terms of sussing out which is the most appropriate design for a particular site? The existing property on the site might or might not help you to decide – it depends on whether it reflects the prevailing character of a particular area.

Planning policies are riddled with comments about 'character of the area' and 'sense of place' because it is the official position of most planning authorities that they don't want their district to look anonymous and so they wanted new houses to reflect what they describe as 'local vernacular traditions'. In most cases, of course, this does not work because there is no such thing as a genuine local vernacular that can be replicated in new developments. Local authorities just end up encouraging developers to build poor modern copies of mass-produced Victorian/Edwardian or general Tudorbethan styled housing. But you generally need a hook to hang the design rationale of your house upon; whether it's an attractive locally-designed house or something more modern that utilises local materials. Whatever you choose, it is likely you will need an argument to justify it in the design and access statement that must accompany your planning application. Most local plans now contain the planning policies in support of environmentally-friendly design. By replacing an old house with a new one you are inevitably improving aspects like energy efficiency and I would recommend making the most of this when seeking to justify the style of your new house.

Comparisons with the existing properties

Because you are applying for a replacement dwelling all the neighbours and the parish council and the planning officers will be tempted to compare what you want now with what already exists on the site. This is often the case and more often than not what exists is pretty unpleasant or you wouldn't be demolishing it! If there is pressure to minimise change by copying what is already there, you need to do take the argument in a direction that suits you. If you are replacing a bungalow then the most obvious comparison to make is with other two-storey houses in the immediate vicinity. If you are replacing a two-storey house make the most of this in your arguments by demonstrating that your proposal is not significantly higher or closer to neighbours etc. It really is horses for courses in terms of arguing and justifying your planning application in the face of potentially hostile neighbours, parish councils and planning officers. Because most areas of the country are characterised by diversity in terms of design styles, heights and proportions, there should be a broad enough palette of choice in the immediate vicinity of your site for you to choose the nature and form of your proposed house to suit you.

Local attitudes

Local attitudes will almost always be involved, so talking to the neighbours is recommended – if only for a quiet life. Taking on board their concerns might be a good idea if it does not compromise your plans but might remove their potential objections. If you are trying to replace a modest bungalow with a much bigger house you might want to think of doing this in several stages, if you have the time. Rather than go all out in the first planning application you could establish the majority of what you want and then increase it with subsequent applications. All this can be done as a paper exercise before you start building anything on the ground.

It is difficult for the planners and the neighbours to raise convincing objections to modest increases in size to an existing approval, even if they would have tried to prevent such a large dwelling initially.

Multiple plots

In looking for your replacement dwelling opportunity you might get lucky, very lucky. There are quite a few small builders and developers who specialise in buying single properties in large grounds with the intention of replacing it not with one, but with several new dwellings. I recommend that you keep your options open. If you can get a building plot yourself and pay for it by selling several others from the same site the whole thing can make a great deal of money.

However, in the topsy-turvy world of planning I would just raise a note of caution. In some areas, notwithstanding the revised advice in PPS 3, local authorities are so devoted to the government's mantra of building 30 dwellings to a hectare (minimum) that if you buy a site with one large house on it and try replacing it with more than one house, you might end up being forced to build lots of smaller units. This may sound okay financially, even if you don't get the building plot you are looking for, but lots of smaller units can mean the site then hits several policy thresholds.

These include the provision of affordable housing and payment of financial contributions towards local infrastructure provision. All of which can seriously undermine the land value and viability of the scheme. It makes sense in the first instance to ensure you understand what thresholds exist in the event that you do find a largish site with real redevelopment potential for more than one house. However, it is important to establish the threshold that a local authority will apply in its requirement for the provision of affordable housing. In some cases in rural areas, this can be as low as two dwellings so if you want to build two then one of them must be an affordable unit. I suspect that policies of this kind are actually just a mechanism for preventing new development in villages, as the prospect of obtaining a meaningful number of affordable units by such draconian thresholds must be about zero.

The replacement of interwar houses with two blocks of flats, entirely in accordance with Government directives for higher densities, but a victim of the planning authorities desire that they must be 'in keeping with the character of the area'. The result is a curious blend of bay windows and squat proportions in a modern building, the architects were forced by planning officers to build no higher than the existing buildings on the site (the outlines in the lower drawing shows the height of the existing houses) and to copy the houses on the left regardless of the architectural consequences. But of course beauty is in the eye...

Demolition

If you have bought a property for demolition and are starting to look for a demolition contractor, stop! Do not demolish anything unless and until you have got planning permission for the replacement first.

Plot developing checklist

Whether or not you create a plot by demolishing the existing one, there are quite a few potential pitfalls to avoid. Checking out the various issues could save you from buying a disaster and steer you in the right direction to a straightforward planning permission and a problem free development.

1.   Right price. Are you paying too much for the plot? Valuing a plot is not an exact science and will ultimately be the most that someone can afford, but that could end up being uneconomic. If you have accurately priced your build costs and have a realistic idea of the value of the resulting house then the land price should be less than the difference between the two. A commercial builder would expect there to be a minimum 20 per cent profit margin. A private self-builder can obviously reduce this margin and this can give you the edge in buying land. In a rising market there is no real risk as a substantial uplift is pretty much guaranteed. But if the market cools and you cut it too fine then the house could end up being worth no more, or even less, than you paid for it. So beware of getting carried away and be realistic about the development costs. Look at the sums in the cold light of day before buying the land.

2.   Outline planning permission. It may sound a bit too obvious to mention but it's vital that the plot you buy has at least got outline planning permission. There are many so-called plots for sale with no permission or with a lapsed planning permission that the seller will claim can be renewed. If there is any doubt about the planning status of the land you should make the purchase subject to the receipt of the permission you want. This can be done either using a legally binding option agreement or by exchanging contracts with completion upon the grant of permission.

It is also extremely important to be clear about what details are included as part of the outline permission. In some cases, in the old style outline permission, it only means that the principle of building a house has been agreed but all detailed issues still need to be granted permission – which entails making another planning application. In cases where the outline permission does not establish the position and size of the house, you have no way of knowing where it will sit on the plot or how big the footprint will actually be. In which case you'll be taking a significant risk, so it makes sense to ensure that the outline permission does at the very least include the access footprint and position of the house.

3   Full planning permission. If your plot has a full permission it will show the detailed design of the house and where it is to be positioned on the site, the access and any garages etc. If this approved scheme is not what you want to build it is perfectly reasonable to make a new application for an alternative size and design of house. Any existing planning permission is unlikely to be the only possible way to develop a plot provided it is in accordance with the planning policies for that area. There are many people who make a living from buying individual plots and adding value by getting a revised approval, often by subdividing them into several plots.

4.   Planning history. Before committing yourself to buying land it is definitely worth investigating the planning history of the plot to find out how controversial the permission was. You can then predict what problems there might be in making an alternative application. The planning file will contain all the objections from neighbours, the parish or town council and the comments of the highway authority. They are all relevant if you intend to buy a plot and change the planning permission.

5.   Surrounding land. The standard land registry search carried out by solicitors will not automatically reveal permissions that might exist for new development surrounding, or even immediately next to, your plot. I have seen purchasers horrified to discover social housing built close to their new house. Large-scale residential schemes or industrial permissions can exist on adjacent land but you will know nothing about them unless you specifically ask. You can ask the additional questions on the search carried out by a solicitor and this will cost a small additional fee, it is also worth you personally visiting the planning department (or their website) to check what permissions have been granted in the surrounding area.

6.   The local plan or local development documents. You may have looked
at the planning history surrounding a plot and decide that it does not
present any problems, but there is still the danger that in time you
could wake up one day with your house in the middle of a housing
development or industrial estate. This is because planning authorities
are targeting many large towns and major villages for additional
housing and commercial developments. They do this by allocating
land through the local plan process. This involves local consultations
and used to take about five years – it remains to be seen if this speeds
up. Either way you could very easily miss the opportunity to comment
or find out what is planned. Because these allocations would not
automatically appear on a solicitor's search it is important to look
at the most recent local plan for that area, usually this will be on the
council's website. Housing and industrial land allocations are closely
related to local and national politics and these do change. You can
never say never, but you can at least minimise the risk. The local plan
contains maps that will also tell you if the plot is in a Conservation
Area; a designation that could have consequences for any alternative
proposal you may be thinking of but which would also help protect the
plot from unattractive future developments nearby.

7   Planning conditions. All planning permissions have conditions attached
to them. These are legally binding and can be restrictive and expensive.
The permission will always be time limited (usually if granted before
2006 for five years from the date it was issued, now three years) so it
is very important to ensure that it is not about to run out. Conditions
may require works to be carried out on land outside the application site
itself – most commonly for the creation of visibility splays to ensure a
safe access. If these splays or the access itself crosses adjoining land, a
failure to agree this with the adjoining landowner could prevent the
development from happening. This is called a ransom and the adjoining
landowner can legitimately require payment in exchange for providing
the vision splays or access across their land. The industry standard for
a ransom payment seems to be around 30 per cent of the development
value of the plot.

Failure to comply with planning conditions is an offence that could lead

to prosecution and it also invalidates the planning permission. This includes situations where development may have been started.

Please also note that renewal of planning consent is not automatic. What was granted under one set of government policies may not be acceptable when those guidelines have changed three or five years later. Or a local objector may raise issues which were not raised at the time of the original application. Allow yourself plenty of time to obtain the renewal. See Tricks of the trade for more details.

8.   Materials. A very common planning condition is to require details of materials to be submitted and agreed. This means that if you buy a plot with permission and hope to build a house inexpensively with render you may get a nasty surprise when the local planning authority requires the local hard-to-find (or rather expensive-to-buy) natural stone. So it sometimes makes sense to establish what materials will be required on a site before buying it to make sure that your financial forecasts and budgets are realistic. Looking at the materials used in surrounding new housing developments is a reasonable way of judging what is likely to be accepted.

9.   Drainage. The availability and costs of providing foul and surface water drainage can vary hugely from one plot to another. It is also a common planning condition to require details of drainage to be agreed and sometimes it will be specified as part of the actual planning permission. The kind a drainage system needed on a plot could have serious cost implications or raised practical problem in providing it. For example, if the ground levels do not allow natural drainage the slab level of the house may need to be increased in height or a pump installed. Establishing the likely costs before the purchase makes sense. Problems in agreeing the drainage system with the local authority drainage engineers or the Environment Agency could also cause delays.

10.   Covenants. The perfect building plot with the perfect planning permission can be rendered valueless it if there is an enforceable covenant on the deeds of the property preventing the erection of the house. It is your solicitor's job to ensure that the title deeds are free from

5

any problems but in my experience you cannot depend on the solicitors alone. There are many covenants, which date back many years and are unenforceable. The original covenant holder or their descendants may be untraceable and have no presence in the area or a covenant may have been breached on other parts of the land and would therefore be incapable of enforcement. It may, as a result, be possible to overcome the cautious advice of a solicitor and obtain covenant indemnity insurance that would then allow you to raise finance, build the house and be covered in the event that the covenant did unexpectedly cause problems. Restrictive covenants can be a problem but they could also present you with an opportunity to buy a plot that others have not had the confidence to tackle.

11.   Rights of way and easements. A building plot can be crossed by both private and public rights of way, which could potentially prevent the implementation of a planning permission or which could, at best, devalue the house. Public rights of way are in theory relatively easy to identify but they will not automatically be indicated in a standard Local Authority Land Registry Search. They should be picked up through the planning process but this cannot be guaranteed. The local authority will have a definitive Rights of Way map showing them and this is available for you to inspect.

Private rights of way are a potential minefield, but if you are lucky they will appear on the deeds of your property, but this is not at all guaranteed. It is therefore important that you physically examine the site for evidence of any apparent longstanding footpaths, which may indicate the existence of personal private rights of access derived by long use. If an individual takes access across private land and is neither permitted nor prohibited from doing so for in excess of 20 years than they may be able to establish a prescriptive right of access.

There is also the potential danger of easements crossing the land for other people's drainage pipes or systems or rights of access for maintaining their adjacent property. For example a major trunk sewer would normally have an easement of three metres either side within, which no development could take place. This would sterilise most building plots.

Checking with the statutory undertakers regarding the existence of any services running across the land is therefore vital.

12. Access rights. You willneed to establish whether the access road to the plot has been adopted by the council as Highways Authority and, if not, then who owns it and what responsibilities might you have for its maintenance? It needs to be clear in your deeds that your plot does have vehicular access rights for all purposes along any unadopted carriageway or private drive. Otherwise you may find that you either do not have vehicular access rights or someone may seek to prevent construction vehicles from getting to your plot. Where land is unregistered, it is important to ensure that these access rights are established before you purchase.

13. Services. One of the advantages of creating a building plot by demolishing an existing house and replacing it is that there will at least be some existing services, such as electricity, gas and mains water etc. If you are looking at a greenfield plot the cost of providing services is something you'll need to take into account and it may well affect the price you can afford to pay for land. If the nearest connection points are some distance away, the companies who provide them can charge a huge amount per metre for the pleasure of extending the pipe or cable to your boundary. It could be much cheaper to offer to lay the pipes yourself and pay for the connection.

14. Boundaries. The ownership of boundaries and boundary disputes fill volumes of legal textbooks so it helps if it's all clear from the outset. I know of perfectly sane and rational people who have fallen out spectacularly over a few inches of their garden where ownership has not been clarified. On deeds there will often be small T-shaped marks that are intended to indicate the direction of nails theoretically pointing to the neighbour's property. This is the historic and traditional way of indicating which is your boundary as the symbolic nails point towards the neighbour who is not responsible for that boundary as they show practically from which side you can maintain it. The worst, and most problematic sort of boundary, is one where it is actually defined by an existing wall of a house, perhaps containing windows.

You may also find that what appears to be a clearly indicated boundary on a local search map is much harder to identify on the ground. I have seen instances where plots are created from dividing gardens where a series of stakes were pushed into the ground to identify the plot when it was being sold. When the transaction was complete the new owners returned to find a fence constructed, which they felt was several feet on their side of where the stakes had been. This can all be avoided now by accurate satellite positioning and I would recommend that, before exchange, you ensure that you check where these co-ordinates are on the ground. Where existing boundary fences are in place, the issue is clearly much simpler and even if the boundaries are in slightly the wrong place – they have probably been there for a very long time and that is what you are getting!

Resolving disputes can require the use of the Party Wall Act. The boundaries of the land you buy may also not define the boundaries of the land that is legally allowed to be used as garden. People are increasingly selling genuine plots with additional areas of agricultural land attached as paddocks and the legal distinction between them can become blurred in the sales particulars. This makes a huge difference as getting planning permission for a larger garden could be impossible and the size of house you will be permitted to build relates to the authorised plot and will not take into account the paddock land you also happen to own. What looks like a large building plot may actually be a very small plot with a large associated field and it should be approached and priced accordingly.

15.   Contaminated land. In researching the planning history of your building plot it may become apparent that there was a previous use, perhaps for commercial or industrial purposes. In which case, contaminated land issues could be relevant. The planning permission might require a Contaminated Land Assessment and clean up, but the absence of such a condition does not guarantee that the land is free of contamination. Therefore, if you have any suspicions about potential contamination problems you could try to ensure that the liability for the cost of any clean-up remains with the vendor. Former petrol filling stations and gasworks sites are classic cases as both involve substances that may have leaked into the ground and require major clean-up operations before you could build a house. There are plots that remain undeveloped because the cost of removing contamination has, until now, rendered them uneconomic.

16.   Noise. It is a real possibility that the apparently tranquil rural plot
      you are considering could actually turn out to be unacceptably noisy.
      I recommend that you visit your potential building plot on various
      occasions at different times of the day and night before buying it.
      Otherwise you may find viewing times arranged in between the goods
      trains or before the gravel workings start up or of after the Boeing 747's
      have passed over! It could come as a nasty shock to hear them when you
      start the building works or move in. Studying the Ordnance Survey map
      can point up potential sources of noise that might make you review your
      decision to buy the plot. This may sound a bit obvious but I have known
      of people who, in their enthusiasm, did not notice noise that later became
      a source of irritation and potential property devaluation.

17.   Flooding. The Environment Agency's website allows you to check
      whether any property is within an identified flood plain. This is
      becoming increasingly important – if only for insurance reasons. If a
      plot was granted planning permission many years ago it may be that
      the flooding issue was not picked up, as it should be today. This is
      particularly relevant if you apply for an alternative planning permission
      once you have bought a site, as the Environment Agency might add a
      condition or even object to a development on flooding grounds – even if
      they hadn't objected in the past.

18.   Neighbouring houses. The position and orientation of neighbouring
      houses could limit your options in developing a plot. The best plots will
      have either no immediate neighbours or ones that are not positioned
      close to boundaries and do not have main windows facing into the site.
      This is because in assessing the acceptability of a proposed new house the
      planners will be concerned to prevent it overlooking or overshadowing
      nearby properties. So when assessing a plot think about what problems
      could be caused to neighbours and how that would constrain the position
      and design of the house you could build. Finding out the tenure of the
      houses nearby can also save potential headaches. If there are Housing
      Association properties in the vicinity you might want to know about it.

19.   Ground conditions and levels. The type of ground you build on has cost
      implications that cannot be ignored. Before you buy it is useful to have a

5

clear idea what they are. A free and effective way of doing this is to talk to the relevant Council Building Regulation Department. The experienced Building Control Officers will have significant local knowledge of developments in that area and an informed understanding of the local ground conditions. If they are not able to provide the assurance you need, or they suggest a problem, an on site assessment may be needed. Sites that have uneven ground levels can provide both opportunities and costs depending on how they are approached. You will need to take changing levels into account in costing your build and in deciding how practical planning permission might be. I have encountered at least one planning permission for a house that could not be built because of the steeply sloping site!

20.   Badgers, bats, newts and archaeology. In addition to all the planning and building regulations that need to be complied with there are sometimes other consents that can cause delays. Plots that contain existing buildings can sometimes be home to endangered bats, and it is an offence to disturb their habitat without permission. Equally, badger sets can cause problems and steps need to be taken to comply with the legislation. I know of one case where a neighbour, who objected to a development, claimed that great-crested newts lived in a pond on the site and held up building by a year. A scheme agreed with the local authority had to be put in place to protect the reptiles whose very existence was a matter of doubt! Some plots may also have archaeological constraints that could require expensive excavations (you may be required to pay for archeologists to carry out an exploratory investigation and possibly more) or that could even prevent the development from taking place. These are uncommon but still worth discounting when looking at a plot, as you can be sure that the local Bat Society or Friends of the Badgers or Local History Group will pop up just as you start building.

Chapter 6

TRICKS OF THE TRADE

Planning is a long-winded bureaucratic process and it is riddled with hidden dangers and opportunities. This section points out some of the most effective tactics and approaches used by people with long experience of playing this game. Because most planning officers seem to see their job as development prevention, it helps to know just what limits there are to their individual influence and control.

For minor proposals the political dimension is becoming more limited as more and more applications are dealt with by planning officers, but this still remains a way of seeking an alternative approach if the planning officers themselves do not agree with your arguments. When things are controversial or large-scale, an ability to communicate with and influence local politicians can be useful

Make friends not enemies

The staff in your local council will be more helpful if you are charming and pleasant, and less helpful if you are not. So the best initial tactic is to be very pleasant to all you come across in the planning department. Very junior members of staff can have an alarming amount of influence in terms of access to the senior officers and they can increase or decrease the speed of response to your enquiries at will. So make friends not enemies. A tactic that really does not work is to go to the council all guns blazing demanding to see the chief planning officer. You would be surprised how many people think it helps. If the planner who eventually gets allocated your application sees you as a nice individual there is a lot they can do to help you avoid a refusal. Not by compromising their professionalism but by keeping you informed about objections, the views of their boss, the likely date of decision and various other things. All of which enable you to respond accordingly.

Keep your emotions in check

A crucial tactic is to care about what you are proposing, but not too much. Whether you are speculating a lot of money on a development site or just building or renovating one house, it all involves a lot of very personal commitment. But it's not possible to negotiate effectively on a planning application if things are taken too personally. A lot of applicants are not sufficiently detached from their plans to be able to stand back, be flexible and play the planning game. If you doubt your ability to retain a degree of detachment from your project you should employ someone to negotiate and deal with the planners on your behalf. Any arguments you may want to make based on your personal circumstances, however heart-rending, will just bore the planners.

Understand which planning policies are relevant

Planning decisions are made, at least in theory, on the basis of policies set out in the relevant development plan documents for a particular district or borough. Understanding which policies are relevant should be your starting point; they will have a powerful influence on which property you buy and what you can build on it.

The trick is to find out what set of policies the planners are actually applying, and whether your application falls foul of them. At any one time there may be several relevant policies, one in the adopted local plan, one in the deposit draft local plan they have abandoned and one being created through the long winded local development framework process. The one you like the sound of may not be the one they are giving most importance to so be sure ask for an explanation as to which plan they are following and why. But don't expect the planning officer to justify on a policy basis every word they say, to require this will be seen as very confrontational and put them on the defensive, so it's normally not worth the hassle.

Know your 'enemy'

All planning departments have some form of hierarchy with less experienced junior planners at the bottom and principal planners at the top. This means that you really need to know the seniority of the person you deal with in order to assess the appropriate weight to be given to what they say. If you ever just pop into a planning department, be very wary of duty officers. The duty officer is taken on a rota basis from within the department. The advice they give should be treated with particular caution.

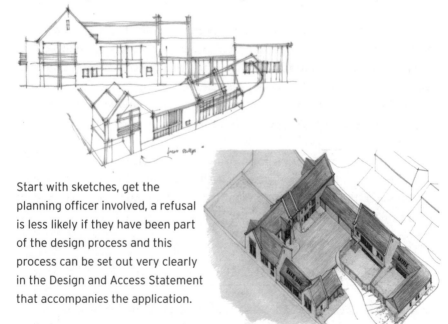

Start with sketches, get the planning officer involved, a refusal is less likely if they have been part of the design process and this process can be set out very clearly in the Design and Access Statement that accompanies the application.

Having a chat with a planning officer

If you have done your research and have an idea of what you intend to build on a particular site then it is perfectly reasonable to arrange to talk to a planning officer about it. A useful tactic is to take in photos of your land or property and have some sketches to discuss, but do not leave them behind or seek written advice. Written advice is never binding on the authority and it may result in an initial negative reaction, which when committed to paper or email will put you on the back foot thereafter. It's better to keep things verbal and as informal as possible so you can assess what issues will need to be dealt with. It's not a bad idea to come in with a lot more than you want – to give the planner the opportunity to do what they often see as their job and knock you back a bit. If the planners can be made to feel part of your team, and it is impressed upon them that their views are important, they are more likely to be friend than foe and they may genuinely have ideas and make suggestions that improve the scheme.

The ratchet effect

Once a development has got planning permission any further applications will be compared with that approval. So any additions or changes will need to be fairly significant to warrant refusal. This means that it is possible to negotiate a series of progressively larger developments on the same site, a tactic I call the ratchet effect. It is up to you which permission you implement on a site; they do not supersede one another.

If you make an application for a proposal but then have to reduce it to get permission, there is a danger that all subsequent applications will be looked at in the knowledge of what was formally negotiated away, so it will be harder to add more.

Push against an open door

It's better to have some of the cake than none at all, particularly if you can come back for seconds. So bearing in mind the ratchet effect, it is often best to get permission on a site even if it is not exactly what you want, than to try and fight for everything all at once. If you have the time to be flexible then there is no need to hang out for every last detail of your chosen design. Better to get most of what you want in the bag with an initial application and then reassess the scheme and reapply with modifications. In this context, it is the cooperative rather then confrontational approach that will usually work best.

Distinguish between principle and detail

A lot of planning decisions are based on the principle of a development, with the details of design etc a secondary consideration. So always be careful not to lose the argument about the principle of building a house on a particular site because it became mixed up with subjective issues like the detailed design. The use of an outline application enables you remove at least some of the fine grain of the design and to focus largely upon establishing the principle of a development. This is an excellent tactic to avoid being dragged into trivia when the value of a site depends largely on establishing agreement that a specified amount of development can, in principle, be built.

Withdrawing an application at the very last minute

If you discover that your application is likely to be recommended refusal, it is often worthwhile waiting for the relevant report to be written before withdrawing the application. This enables you to see in clear terms the logic behind the planners concerns. It also enables you to decide whether or not to proceed with the refusal and then a planning appeal or whether to negotiate. Where an application is recommended for approval and goes before a planning committee it is still possible for the committee to overrule the officers and refuse it. If you do not want to have a black mark against the property or you would like to continue negotiating on a scheme it is possible to withdraw the application at the very last minute, actually at the planning committee after the resolution to refuse has been made. This is because a planning decision has not been formally made until the decision notice is physically printed and issued. This is a little-known area of planning law that is not exploited enough by people who want to avoid a refusal and who assume that because planning committee has voted on an application that it is then too late to withdraw it. It isn't.

Negotiate with neighbours

They may be unfriendly and positively spiky but is often worth embracing the neighbours. People have an understandable opposition to change and live in fear of property devaluation. In my opinion very few objections to applications are based on genuine planning issues, they normally reflect more emotive or financial concerns. So the solution to put it rather crudely may be to buy off the opposition by solving their problems as part of the development. For example, new boundary treatments, the felling or planting of trees or minor redesigns to accommodate their concerns can be worth doing if it makes a development proposal less contentious. Although a slight word of caution, be careful not to overreact to neighbours who may have unjustified and irrational objections that would have little influence on planners who already support the scheme.

Persistence

There are many different ways of developing a particular site. Over time, planning policies change and planning circumstances can improve, so persistence can pay off. This is not a recommendation to bang your head against a policy brick wall but rather to keep an open mind about how the site can be developed and over what timescales. The government has introduced powers enabling local authorities to decline to determine repeated applications that are similar. This is an attempt to prevent endless and usually pointless proposals being submitted successively on the same site in the hope that objectors will eventually be worn down. This new power does not prevent the submission of alternative schemes that incorporate different approaches to design or for different types of development. As in most areas of life, persistence is ultimately omnipotent.

Planning gain

Extracting money from development sites to pay for local infrastructure is currently a matter of heated debate. The government is threatening to introduce a new development land tax called a 'planning gain supplement' that will seek to take some of the added land value generated by planning permissions. This is likely to be in addition to the more familiar planning agreements under section 106 of the planning act that are necessary to pay for costs directly associated with the development. These include the provision of affordable housing in accordance with adopted policies; financial contributions towards additional school places were there will be additional children; vital contributions towards creating additional traffic capacity to deal with extra traffic and other direct consequences of a scheme. Increasing numbers of local authorities have supplementary planning guidance and documents that set out their criteria for working out planning gain contributions. This results in a pro rata tax per dwelling, which has the twin benefits of being predictable and fair.

However, in cases where they do not apply a roof tax approach, rather than just accepting without argument the amounts of money that they demand, it may be well worth seeking to negotiate the amount downwards. Equally there are many instances where generous planning gain contributions to local facilities can tip the balance in favour of a scheme. This is not the buying of a planning permission; it is recognising the need for local community facilities that may be a material planning consideration in the overall assessment of the impact of a development proposal and could, therefore, put the balance in favour. The government recently issued a suggested standard pro forma for section 106 agreements that might prove to be useful.

Planning law

Changes in planning law can have profound consequences for the implementation of planning policies and planning permissions. Changes can result from government legislation or case law. It pays to be up to date with what's happening because, as one loophole or opportunity closes, others tend to open up in unexpected ways. Keeping an eye on the planning press and subscribing to professional information services can be worth the expense.

Political awareness

I have placed a lot of emphasis on local politics in understanding the nature of planning. Spending some time getting a handle on the political dynamics of a particular local authority can pay dividends when you're trying to get permission. You may encounter helpful and switched-on planning officers who will not only tell you their own professional opinions but also indicate their understanding of the, perhaps, rather different political aspirations and concerns of members of the planning committee.

Avoidance of risk

The majority of developers avoid exposure to unacceptable levels of risk either by buying land at around its current value, to be followed by an average payment, or by making a purchase that is subject to the receipt of satisfaction planning permission. A planning refusal is only a disaster if you have risked serious money trying to achieve it; this risk can be minimised through the use of options and conditional contracts. The ultimate goal of course is to buy freehold land inexpensively and speculatively, with the confidence that permission for development will be forthcoming. Such sites are hard to find.

Understanding the fallback position

The planning decision-maker is required in law to take into account the fallback position in respect of any development site. This means the development, which may happen anyway, could be a previously consented scheme or it could be permitted development. The fallback position will often establish a set of parameters on a site in terms of the nature and consequences arising from the implementation or continuation of alternative uses or development. For example, if a site could in any event generate large amounts of traffic, this has to be weighed in the balance when the Highway Authority makes a traffic assessment of a development proposal that will generate the same amount or less. A point to note about the fallback position is that its importance as a material issue is to some extent dependent upon the likelihood of it occurring

Ian Sullivan Architectural Design Ltd.
Swindon. 01793 612663

Presentation is all, the nicer the picture the more likely you are to get a permission

Use the right planning consultant

Choosing the right people to be in your development team is always going to be critically important. The choice of planning consultant may not be the obvious one. Be cautious about employing a planner in the area of the local authority that he or she has only just left. Their former colleagues may still be friendly but they will also be desperate to avoid appearing too friendly or to be doing any favours or giving special treatment to that individual. So rather than having an easier ride on the planning front it could make things harder. Equally, using a local planning consultant who has very good relationships with local planning officers may not be wise if you anticipate a degree of conflict. The locally based, one-man band planning consultant may have an ongoing working relationship with the local authority that is more important than the relationship with you. They will be reluctant to upset those planners and this may influence the extent to which your scheme is aggressively pursued in the face of local opposition. Like it or not, planning can be about individual personalities as well as policies and politics.

Solve technical problems before submission

Because planning authorities are under such pressure to meet targets, and the timescales are very limited, it is advisable to deal with all possible technical issues and resolve potential problems prior to submitting the application. For example, the access design and highways concerns of drainage issues, desktop archaeological investigations, trees, rights of way, flood risk assessments etc should all have been sorted with the relevant outside organisations prior to submission. It is perfectly acceptable and reasonable to approach those who will be consulted on an application before it is submitted to try and forestall any potential problems. If you can get the written agreement to your scheme from such bodies, include copies with your planning application.

Avoiding problems with renewals

Until recently there was a general belief that consent would be renewed as a matter of course. This wasn't a sound assumption as some permissions no longer conformed with planning policies. However, since August 23, 2006 that is academic as planning authorities are now unable to grant an extension to any planning consent or renew it without a new application being submitted with no guarantee that it will be granted.

One of the tricks which has traditionally been used to avoid a consent expiring is to start building. Many developers achieved this by doing the bare minimum to demonstrate that work has begun on site. The popular mechanism for this has been digging and filling footings, connecting services or undertaking minimal highways work. However, in recent years this has proven a more difficult feat to manage, particularly with the need to have conditions discharged prior to undertaking works on site. It is therefore essential to establish with the local planning department what is required on site to satisfy development criteria.

Under the Planning and Compulsory Purchase Act 2004, the standard length of a consent granted after August 25, 2005 was reduced from five years down to three. This is a much tighter timescale in which to either progress work or arrange any changes to the consent (especially if the consent has been purchased and the clock is already ticking). See 'The ratchet effect' earlier in this chapter.

Chapter 7

THE PLANNING PROCESS

This chapter deals with the processing of an application once it is submitted to the planning authority, but it's important to be aware that the administrative aspect of this game is only part of the story. The route to getting permission does not begin with the submission of a planning application and it does not finish once you've got your written notice of permission. It starts when you decide to embark upon a development project, because all the decisions you make from that point on will influence your chances of success.

The actual processing of an application by the local authority is fairly straightforward and breaks down into a series of steps, but it is vital that you can predict any problems before they arise to ensure that you clear all the possible obstacles.

You will need to establish the planning policy context in which your proposal will be assessed and the on-site characteristics and constraints that may influence the design solutions you arrive at. You may wish to take advantage of the advice that can be available from local authorities in the hope that the application you submit will meet their expectations. But pre-application advice can be a mixed blessing. Some local authorities are able to give real expert guidance, while others give out very superficial, and potentially misleading, advice. I know some developers who treat their first application on a particular site as the means of acquiring realistic planning advice. This works on the basis that the eight weeks spent by the authority on their application is likely to provide a more helpful steer than endless pre-application discussions with a planning officer who then leaves.

On the basis that you have dealt with all the technical issues and can present a scheme of a design that you believe will meet the relevant planning policy objectives, and that deals with on-site planning considerations, you may then submit it and the bureaucratic process will commence.

From the submission of your application to receiving a decision should take no longer than eight weeks for a minor proposal and 13 weeks for a major development. The planners are under real pressure to meet these timescales. The government has come up with a clever wheeze of effectively linking a council's performance to the financing of planning departments. This means that people's jobs are at stake if they don't deal with things quickly. Speed, of course, does not encourage negotiations during the life of an application. In the past, planners might have been happy to look at plans to overcome problems but they are the much less likely to do so now.

As far as the local planning authority is concerned, planning is now a process-driven activity, the outcomes of the decisions are less important than the speed and procedures followed in reaching them. They would never like to admit this and continue to bang on about quality, but the reality is that government target setting is driving the system not the individual chief planning officer's good intentions.

The procedure

The processing of your application will involve the following stages:
■ The application will be checked to ensure that forms are properly completed, plans included, the owner and/or leaseholder of the property (if not you) notified and the correct fee paid.

■ If all is correct, the application will be 'registered' and allocated a number.

■ The application will be advertised to ensure that people know about it. This may involve some or all of the following: newspaper adverts, notices placed on the site of the proposal and letters sent to neighbouring houses. The site notice must be in place for at least 21 days and it is the responsibility of the planning authority to erect it, although they may well request that the applicant does this. The efforts made to involve the public in this process will be set out in the Statement of Community Involvement that is one of the development plan documents in the new local development framework.

■ Consultations will be carried out. This will include notifying the parish or town council, the local Highways Authority, and other public bodies who supply services such as water or drainage.

■ A planning officer will be allocated your application. He or she will consider it against existing council policies and any past history of decisions relating to your house or similar houses in the area. The council will often have standards, which will need to be satisfied for things like parking provision, visibility near road junctions etc.

■ The planning officer will visit the site.

■ The planning officer will make a recommendation of refusal or approval. He or she may request that you withdraw the application so that it can be modified to incorporate changes, if they feel problems can be overcome – although you can't always depend on this helpful approach.

■ The decision will be made by the chief officer responsible for planning matters, or the application will be considered by a planning committee made up of locally elected councillors. If objections are raised to the application it would generally be reported to a committee. The planning committee may wish to make a site visit. The decision will then be made at the committee's next meeting.

■ Once the application has been determined, you will receive a decision notice that will be subject to various binding conditions.

Planning on the web

All local planning authorities now have websites that include sections dealing with planning. They will usually include links to the local planning policy documents and an increasing number allow you to search their

planning application databases to look at current and historic applications. The government is putting a lot of pressure on councils' for planning services to be delivered electronically, even to the point of electronically submitting applications. The government-sponsored planning website www. planningportal.gov.uk provides a mechanism to submit applications to a large number of authorities. It also includes a lot of useful planning policy and procedural information. It appears to be a potential monopoly being fattened up for sale to the private sector, we shall see. Meanwhile, it's worth looking at, as are local authority websites, as a way of tracking an application through the process, checking out policies and researching planning histories.

Who is consulted on an application?

Once the local authority has registered the application it then consults a list of organisations both internal and external. A decision will not be made until a 21-day consultation period has expired. They will consult neighbours by letter or by putting up a site notice. The local parish or town council will be consulted along with highway engineers, the Environment Agency and even the council's professional archaeologist. If the house or plot is in a conservation area, the council's conservation officer will also be involved. It is now required that the Environment Agency is consulted before an application is submitted where a site is on land liable to flood.

In Circular 08/2005, the government explains the duty of statutory consultees to respond to consultations on planning applications within the set time period. The applicants and local authority also have a duty to provide sufficient information. All of which sounds very sensible and helpful except that the word respond is open to many and varied interpretations. A holding objection is a response; a request for more information is a response. The reality of these provisions, in common with most process-based reforms, seems to be to simply add to and relocate the delay so that it is outside the measured time period. So statistically things seem faster, in reality they are slower.

Any one of the numerous professionals who are consulted could stick a spanner in the works and delay your application or cause it to be refused. So my advice is to talk to the people who are going to be consulted before they get the letter from the council. Talk to the neighbours, discuss the access with the Highway Authority and get the views of the conservation officer if necessary. This could make a real difference to the outcome.

What criteria will be used to judge a proposal?

This is a very big question; but government policies, the regional special strategies and local development documents will all be relevant to some degree. The question can only really be answered simplistically in relation to small-scale proposals.

Applications for extensions and other domestic developments will usually be judged on the basis of:

■ The planning authority's own planning policies and government policy.

■ The history of planning decisions related to the property in question and its neighbourhood.

■ The effect of what is proposed upon the residential environment of neighbouring houses.

■ The suitability of the design and appearance of the extension relative to the character of the house and its surroundings.

■ Whether the new property, commercial development or extension will affect the amount of parking spaces required or available, or affect highway safety.

Who makes the decision?

Applications are determined either by a planning committee made up of elected councillors or by the most senior planner, the chief planning officer. A decision made by the chief planning officer is known as a decision made under delegated authority. The government has put a target in place to encourage 90 per cent of the decisions made by local authorities to be made under delegated powers not by committees of councillors. This is a double-edged sword as it means that councillors may interfere less perhaps resulting in greater predictability for prospective developers but it also means that the planning officers and bureaucrats wield considerable individual discretion, influence and, ultimately, power.

If an application is put before committee there will usually be a recommendation made by a planning officer as to how it should be determined.

Relatively large-scale proposals such as developments of groups of houses or commercial schemes of thousands of square metres may still be dealt with under delegated powers. Only if there is real controversy will house extensions or single new houses be put before a committee. For a small-scale development to be considered by committee there would normally need to be more than one objection from a neighbour or the parish council, town council, or even a member of the planning committee itself would need to request it.

Planning committee meetings are open to the public but only a limited number of planning authorities allow either objectors or applicants to speak at them.

How long does it take?

Local authorities have a duty under the legislation to determine applications within eight weeks. In practice, different authorities have varying success in working within this time limit but they are all ruthless in trying. Unless it is withdrawn for new amended plans to be submitted most minor applications should be determined within the eight week period, but that might mean a refusal for reasons that could have been overcome had there been more time.

Before you submit the application

Overcoming objections by talking to your neighbours and ensuring that the design and appearance of your proposal is satisfactory to the planners during pre-application discussions is the most effective way of reducing the time and hassle involved in the process.

A planning application is likely to be most successful if the planners are considered as one of the team involved in the development proposal. The team is made up of you, the applicant, the person drawing the plans, the various outside bodies that are consulted on technical aspects of a proposal such as the Highways Authority, the Environment Agency and the planner. The person who draws up the proposal is faced with the task of reconciling the, sometimes conflicting, requirements of the applicant, consultees, planner and building regulations.

If you decide that some informal advice from the planners might be helpful, the following tactics will be useful.

■ When you have decided roughly what you wish to do - whether it is a multiple plot scheme, single new house, an extension, new garage, moving your boundary fence or whatever - take relevant photographs. Also have your designer draw some initial sketches and make an appointment to discuss the proposals with an appropriate level of planning officer. You will receive informal verbal advice as to the likely acceptability of what you wish to do. This is the stage at which complete non-starters may be eliminated.

■ It is best that the pre-application advice is only obtained in verbal form. Informal written comments are likely to be less flexible and may amount to a hasty, partial assessment of your proposal. This could have an influence upon the formal consideration of the actual planning application. You may be tempted to leave a copy of the initial proposal for the planning officer to consider and to discuss with their colleagues. However, this is not advisable because the first design or layout is unlikely to be an accurate or sophisticated representation of what is desired and could lead to an unnecessarily negative response. A site meeting to discuss your proposal is probably the best method of gauging the likelihood of an approval. Unfortunately, not all planning authorities have the resources or inclination to provide such a service. Photographs offer a reasonable alternative.

Consider carefully the advice you have received. The experience and skill of your designer and knowledge and experience of your planning adviser, if you have one, will be very important in distinguishing between the preferences and requirements spelled out by the planner. "We would prefer," is not quite the same as "It is essential that," and the language used is rarely that straightforward.

Submitting the application

■ The application will not be registered unless it is complete, including the Design and Access Statement if required, and the forms correctly filled in. At this stage, telephone the planning department to find out when it would be convenient to go into the planning department and have your application checked by a planning officer. Having the application checked prior to submission saves time involved in amending anything once it has been received. The application is checked for its completeness. No judgment is made as to its acceptability as a proposal.

■ Once you have been informed that the application is registered, keep a note of the application number and find out the name of the planning officer who is dealing with it. You can probably look this up on the council's web site.

■ You should feel free to contact the planning officer handling your case to discuss its progress and to give any additional information needed. (Try not to pester the planning officer, though, and wait for a few weeks after you have submitted the application before you contact them). Any number of amendments, additional information or revisions may be needed to the design or siting to make the proposal acceptable. Pre-application advice is not binding on an authority and many seem to forget that they have given any; a problem not helped by high staff turnover. Try to ensure that you withdraw the application rather than let it be refused. If it's a large scheme of 10 or more houses then the 13-week period may allow some negotiations during the process. However, even if this is not possible it would be unreasonable of them not to explain the nature of any problems if you contact them, thereby giving you an opportunity to amend or withdraw the proposal accordingly.

■ It may happen that, despite the informal advice you received initially and your willingness to make minor revisions to the proposal, your plan is recommended for refusal. Find out exactly what the problem is. If the application is certain to be recommended for refusal then it may be sensible to withdraw it at the last minute. This will enable you to start the negotiations afresh. Withdrawing the application prevents a refusal notice being issued, which could devalue the land and perhaps prejudice future negotiations or consideration by the authority.

■ Don't start work until you have actually received the permission notice. Remember that anything anybody says during the whole procedure carries no actual weight in terms of the decision until you have actually got the written decision notices in your hands. This can be extremely frustrating. Whatever advice you receive from the planning officer dealing with your application, the councillors or the chief planning officer may wish to overrule it, and they can do so legitimately.

If your application is refused, reasons will be given and you must decide whether or not to appeal against them. If it is approved, conditions will often be attached.

What assistance is available?

Planning departments are usually open during normal office hours Monday to Friday and can help in the following ways:

■ Current and past planning applications are available for you to inspect either on their website or at their offices, the latter usually by appointment.

■ Professional planning officers are available to answer your enquiries and to advise you by phone, at the planning office or possibly on site. All departments have their own systems and appointments are sometimes necessary. Increasingly, you will find it hard to speak to a senior planner and you will be palmed off with a very junior, inexperienced individual who is terrified of saying too much and getting into trouble. Faced with anything like a complex or difficult question the response is normally that you have to write in. This is very frustrating when you can be almost certain that there is an experienced senior Officer in the building who could answer your question straight off.

■ Many planning departments produce free guidance documents and leaflets for the public to assist them in making applications. They are available on their websites or at the council offices.

■ The planning and building regulations application forms are available from the website, or can be collected at the council offices or posted to you.

Please remember, when dealing with planning officers, that many are just trying to do a difficult job as well as they can in difficult circumstances. So be friendly, be polite and don't be afraid to ask questions even if the person appears unwilling to answer them.

Although the legal responsibilities of all planning departments are the same, and the process driven targets imposed by the government affect them all, the quality of service to the public and the speed of service given can vary enormously throughout the country.

What sort of decision can be made?

1. Your application may be approved, subject to certain conditions. In some areas copies of the plans that have been approved are sent back to the applicant so there can be no doubt as to what has been agreed.

2. Your application may be refused. If so, the reasons will be listed on the decision notice.

3. Your application may be recommended for approval subject to you entering into a legally binding agreement regarding a particular aspect of the proposal. For example, to provide a drainage system or off-site highway improvements, or to make financial contributions towards affordable housing or education provision in the locality. This Section 106 agreement will relate to the property, not just to the person who enters into it.

(Some authorities will resolve to grant permission following the completion of the agreement. Others only resolve to authorise the chief planner to grant permission following the agreement. In the latter case, the authority has still got the right not to grant permission should circumstances change between the consideration of the application and the signing of the agreement).

Conditions

There is always a condition on a grant of planning permission that the development permitted must commence within a certain period of time. For a full permission, it was usually five years but the standard time limit is now three years. There are rarely conditions, which demand that the development should be completed within a certain time. In most cases, once a development has been started in compliance with the conditions, the permission cannot expire. A development will normally be considered to have started once foundation work has commenced in accordance with the necessary building regulations.

Permissions will often be subject to conditions in addition to the time limit. An example would be the condition that the materials to be used, the bricks and tiles, must be agreed or in the case of an extension that they should match the existing materials. Another common condition is that there should be adequate car parking available where, for instance, there are on-street parking problems. If you are unclear what any condition means, ask the planning department.

You may appeal against conditions that you feel are unreasonable. However, in so doing you are opening up the entire permission for reconsideration and ultimately the whole thing could be refused.

Some conditions will demand that you do certain things (such as plant trees) 'In accordance with a scheme that shall be submitted to and approved in writing by the Planning Authority'. In these cases, and others where it is not clear exactly what is required, get agreement in writing from the planning department that each condition has been met after you have finished the work (or before if necessary). This is in your interest, as you can be prosecuted and ultimately fined for failure to implement conditions.

Making an application on land you do not own

It is quite in order for someone to make a planning application on land which does not belong to them and over which they have no control, provided that they notify in writing those who have an 'interest' in the land, usually the owner. This notification is done by means of a form called a Section 66 certificate, which must be completed when submitting a planning application.

This ability does give rise to confusion and people sometimes feel intimidated

or offended if they are informed that someone is seeking permission on their land. However, gaining planning permission has no influence whatsoever over land ownership or the control of land. Just because a developer gains planning permission to build a house in your garden does not influence the fact that it is your garden. What is more, planning permission relates to the land (or buildings) not to the applicant (unless it is specifically personal consent, which is rare). This means you may implement a permission relating to your house that was gained by another person, e.g. a previous owner.

Applications affecting boundaries

The Party Wall Act is likely to be relevant and a leaflet about this will be provided by the planning department. You require your neighbours' consent to build on their land, which includes foundations and overhanging eaves, guttering or downpipes. You will also need their consent to enter their land to enable buildings on or close to the boundary to be built. It is sometimes possible to build from within a site, but it is simpler and quicker to have all round access.

The ownership and alignment of property boundaries is shown on deeds, usually held by mortgage companies.

Permission will be needed via party wall considerations for development within a set distance from a legally defined party wall and for the use of a neighbour's wall to tie into, or building an extension where a wall is not in joint ownership. Remember that planning permission does not remove any private legal rights or responsibilities regarding ownership or access rights.

Land ownership

To ascertain the ownership of land is usually a simple matter, although this is not always the case as not all land is registered. The land registry records are open to the public and they can be accessed online or by filling in a form sent with the appropriate fee that will provide the required information. To obtain the address of the relevant land registry for your area, contact the land charges section of your local council.

Chapter 8
MAKING A PLANNING APPLICATION

Who do I apply to?

The relevant planning departments are currently found in the planning authority of the area, in which the development site is situated, which may be:

England and Wales
The relevant planning departments are currently found within the local authority for the area in which the development site is situated, which may be:

■ District councils
■ Borough councils
■ City councils
■ National park authorities.
■ Unitary authorities

Scotland
■ District authorities
■ Highland regional councils
■ City councils

Who should design your scheme and draw the plans?

There are many people who design extensions etc and draw plans for planning applications. They include professional architects, architectural technicians, builders, surveyors and many others.

The ability and experience of the person you choose will have a direct bearing on the quality of the building created and value for money that is obtained. It can also have a strong bearing on the success, or otherwise, of your application. Experience in the right field is essential. Some architects are familiar with the requirements of volume house builders, some are better suited to bespoke one-off houses, and others are best used for simple extensions and domestic applications.

Your plans, elevations and artist's impressions will, in many cases, be all that the planners and planning committee have to go on. If your project is well presented and shows your proposal in the best light, it is commonsense that your chance of success will be improved.

Be aware that planning departments have their favorite architects, not in the sense of corruption but just because they have seen some designers come up with what they want on many occasions and trust them. If you can work out whose designs are most successful in terms of successful applications in a particular authority it can give you a real advantage.

When establishing the fees for any project, it is important to ensure that you understand clearly what services and plans are included. For example does the fee include all revised plans necessary to obtain planning, including, if necessary, a revised application and building regulation approval?

Choosing someone to design the proposal

The ability and experience of the person you choose will have a direct bearing on the chances of getting permission, the marketability of the development created and land value and profit obtained.
It is important that the person you employ should demonstrate:

■ A successful track record
■ Examples of previous work, now built

■ An understanding of your priorities not just of their own designs
■ A willingness and desire to understand what you want out of the proposal in financial terms
■ A serious commitment to achieving planning permission through negotiations and flexibility

The best way to find a designer is by personal recommendation. The second best way is to ask another developer who has been successful locally, or to ask an established local builder. It makes sense to use a designer who knows the way the local planning office works – it can make the whole planning process a lot smoother.

I cannot emphasise too much that, when establishing the cost of the project, you understand clearly what services the fee includes, such as all revised plans necessary to obtain planning and building regulations approval.

Can I draw the plans myself?

Even with the most minor proposals, most people do not have the knowledge or ability to draw the plans required to make a planning application. The plans required to make a building regulations application are even more difficult to produce. As a result, having plans professionally drawn is usually advisable.

If you have technical drawing or Cad skills, and when building regulations are not required such as for a conservatory or the development is very small and is to be dealt with using the card notification system of building control, then drawing the plans yourself may be possible. Having a copy of the original plans for your house could make it a fairly simple exercise if you can draw accurately with a scale rule.

When making an application for a conservatory, it may be possible to get away with a location plan, site plan and photographs of the house and copies of the manufacturer's literature. Some authorities will accept this so it could be worth a try. If they don't, you have only lost some time.

Choosing an agent

You will probably get a designer or an architect to draw your plans, but who should represent you and negotiate with the planners? It is fair to say that most architects know as much about planning as most planners know about architecture, which is a bit but not enough to do it. So a planning consultant can be a good idea, although avoid confrontational types who are bullish about going to appeal.

But also be cautious about local agents who appear to be buddies with the planning department, they are in danger of valuing their long term relationship with the planners more than their short term relationship with you. A good agent has the advantage of being one step away from the project emotionally, not only being able to stay cool under pressure and saving you time but also having a fresh set of eyes that can bring a different, potentially very constructive approach, to problems that are encountered.

Types of application

A householder application for a straightforward domestic extension or garage will be a full application, which means it provides all the details of what is proposed. The different types of application are described below:

1. Full applications

If you wish to seek approval for both the principle of a development and the design and other details of the proposal. Full permission is always required if you wish to make a change of use application.

2. Outline and reserved matters applications

If you are looking for a plot, or have ever bought land, you will have heard the phrase 'outline planning application'. This is a planning permission which contains only a limited amount of information about what can be built on a site. It establishes the principle of development land without specifying all of the details; they are reserved for future consideration as part of a reserved matters (RM) application. In this case the permission is effectively given in two halves, or as an alternative can be applied for all at once as a full application.

As of June 2006, the outline application has been effectively killed off. The two-stage process is still allowed but the amount of information required is radically increased.

Reserved matters previously consisted of siting, design, external appearance, means of access and the landscaping of the site. These will remain in use as part of current permissions until they have expired.

New reserved matters permissions have now been changed to:

Layout: The way in which buildings, routes and open spaces are provided within the development and their relationship to buildings and spaces outside the development.

Scale: The height, width and length of each building proposed in relation to its surroundings.

Appearance: The aspects of a building or place, which determine the visual impression it makes, excluding the external built form of the development.

Access: The accessibility to and within the site for vehicles, cycles and pedestrians in terms of the positioning and treatment of access and circulation routes and how these fit into the surrounding access network.

Landscaping: The treatment of private and public space to enhance or protect the site's amenity through hard and soft measures. For example, through planting of trees or hedges or screening by fences or walls. All of the above sound fairly reasonable, however, where an outline application used to include a limited number of the reserved matters, from now on all outline applications must include the following:

Use: The use or uses proposed for the development and any distinct development zones within the site identified.

Amount of development: The amount of development proposed for each use.

Indicative layout: An indicative layout with separate development zones proposed within the site boundary where appropriate.

Scale parameters: An indication of the upper and lower limits for height, width and length of each building within the site boundary.

Indicative access points: An area or areas in which the access point or points to the site will be situated.

In practical terms, it will not be possible to generate this level of detailed information without having first designed the scheme for the site. The key aspect of outline permission, its simplicity, has been removed by requiring so much detail at the initial stage. The combination of scale parameters, amount of development and indicative layout leave very little undecided except perhaps the shape of the windows and colour of the bricks!

So I would recommend that, unless it is a significant development proposal of more than ten houses, you should be prepared to make full applications and arrange your land purchases accordingly.

3. Temporary permission

If you require approval for change of use or other works for a specific short-term period only.

4. Relaxation of conditions

If you wish to apply to relax a condition, or conditions, of a previous permission. You cannot often reasonably apply to relax a condition once you have started a development, if that condition is a prerequisite to the acceptability of the scheme.

5. Renewal of planning permission

A planning permission can only be renewed where consent has not expired. No plans are required, just the fee and ownership certificate with covering letter, but you cannot guarantee it will be approved - see Chapter 6, Tricks of the Trade. It is no longer possible to renew an application by varying the time limit condition.

The planning application

A planning application consists of a set of complicated forms (provided by the planning department) and a set of plans of the proposal (provided by you) and the appropriate fee.

The fee

The current fee (2007) charged by local planning authorities is £135 for an application for an extension or other domestic proposals and £265 per house. If an outline application is made, regardless of the number of proposed houses, the fee is based on the site area at £265 per 0.1 of a hectare or part thereof.

The design and access statement

At the same time as doing away with the simplicity and relatively low cost of the outline planning application, the government has introduced another major time delay and cost to the process. More or less all applications (other than extensions to existing houses, changes of use and advert applications) must now be accompanied by a Design and Access

Statement. This is how the government describes them:

'One statement should cover both design and access, allowing applicants to demonstrate an integrated approach that will deliver inclusive design, and address a full range of access requirements throughout the design process. A Design and Access Statement is a short report accompanying and supporting a planning application to illustrate the process that has led to the development proposal, and to explain and justify the proposal in a structured way.'

'Development proposals that are not based on a good understanding of local physical, economic and social context are often unsympathetic and poorly designed, and can lead to the exclusion of particular communities. A major part of a Design and Access Statement is the explanation of how local context has influenced the design.'

How or why the average developer or builder is compelled to take into account the economic and social context of a location is not at all clear. Suffice to say that it will now be necessary to employ a planning consultant or architect to produce a justification for what you want to build, which will add at least £500 to your costs.

The government blurb continues:
'Design and Access Statements will allow local communities, access groups, amenity groups and other stakeholders to involve themselves more directly in the planning process without needing to interpret plans that can be technical and confusing. This will help to increase certainty for people affected by development and improve trust between communities, developers and planners. It will also enable the design rationale for the proposal to be more transparent to stakeholders and the local planning authority.'

This can surely only have been written by someone with zero experience of attempting to get planning permission. We all know full well that the vast majority of people simply want to prevent new houses being built anywhere near them and they will use any avenue open to them to try and stop developments.

The local authority now has the power to refuse to entertain an application

unless it is accompanied by a design and access statement. Another justification for delay and another reason for refusal, no doubt.

We are advised that the design component of the statement must include justification and explain the design principles and concepts that have been applied to particular aspects of the proposal – these are the amount, layout, scale, landscaping and appearance of the development.

All of which will be based on an assessment of the site's immediate and wider context in terms of physical, social and economic characteristics and relevant planning policies.

The access component of this statement should 'explain how access arrangements will ensure that all users will have equal and convenient access to buildings and spaces and the public transport network.' The statement should address the need for flexibility of the development and how it may adapt to changing needs.

What this will all mean in practice is difficult to predict. It will take time to see how strictly local authorities interpret this – in particular for the large number of simple single or multiple plot developments that are often built in standard residential areas in which the design component is based on fitting in with surrounding development and where the need for lots of explanation is minimal. For those who want to read the full text of this elevating tome it is called Circular 01 of 2006 listed on the website www.communities.gov.uk under planning policies.

Application form questions

The government is currently consulting on a nationwide set of application forms but at present planning departments tend to have their own design. It is possible to fill in forms on the planning portal website and either print them off or send them to the local authority electronically. The questions asked are always very similar. Some departments provide simplified forms used in householder applications only. I have considered some typical questions below.

Questions 1 & 2: Name & address of applicant & agent

If the name and address of an agent is given, all correspondence from the department will be sent to that agent. It will be useful to give a contact name. If you use an agent the local authority is unlikely to accept a change of agent half way through unless the original agent formally instructs the council that they have handed the case back to you or to someone else. So if you fall out with an agent mid way through, things can get tricky. In the absence of any agent, remember to give your daytime / mobile telephone number and email address.

Question 3: Site address

This will usually be your address, but remember that you can make a planning application in relation to property that you do not own. This is helpful should you wish to buy a house but want to make the purchase subject to a successful application to extend it.

Question 4: What is the application for?

This should be a clear, simple description of what is proposed. Describe the number of storeys and the position in relation to the existing house (rear, side or front). The local authority is not allowed to change the description without your express consent. Do not agree to do this if it matters, for example they might want to change an application for a detached annexe in your garden into a single dwelling. Only accept a change if the description still reflects exactly what you propose.
Examples:
- Single storey detached garage in rear garden
- Two storey side extension
- Front facing pitched roofed dormer window
- Residential development of five detached two-storey dwellings
- Change of use from (B1) office into three flats

Question 5: Plans and drawings

The type of plans and drawings that are required are considered in detail below. On the forms you should list and describe the type of plan and its scale.

For example: location plan (1:1250), site plan (1:500) and elevations (1:100).

Question 6: Will proposed materials match the existing?

This answer is only relevant to extensions and should normally be yes.

Question 7: Is the site boundary to be altered?

On most applications, the boundary will follow the same line, but if you wish to increase the size of a garden area by enclosing agricultural land or by enclosing an area of public open space provided on a housing estate, then this will in itself require planning permission. So if the answer to this question is yes, it should usually be reflected in question four.

Question 8: Drainage

Drainage is becoming an increasingly important issue. By the time you are filling in these forms you should have the drainage solution all buttoned up and have agreed non-mains drainage, and anything problematic, in advance with the Environment Agency. All new buildings containing new kitchens or bathrooms should have separate connections to the foul water sewer, and all new roof connections to a storm water sewer. So before you start, locate the position of the nearest drains and sewers as building over them or diverting them creates extra work which can be so expensive as to render some developments uneconomic. The building regulations department of the local council should be able to give some initial helpful advice, as they will be familiar with the local area and hopefully any well-known local drainage problems.

Question 9: Are there any trees to be felled?

Planning authorities will wish to see trees retained wherever possible. You would be wise to investigate whether any trees you wish to remove are protected by a tree preservation order. Think very carefully about trees before making contact with the local authority concerning your development ideas, even at the earliest stages. They can serve a TPO very quickly and as a precautionary measure. That might not be the end of the world but it could at the very least add complications and delays in the progress of your application. If the planning authority considers an attractive tree is in any way threatened, because for example they understand a property has changed hands or they receive enquiries about a site following or during probate, or following its marketing, then it can serve an emergency tree protection order literally in hours.

Remember that special kinds of foundations can be laid which will not damage tree roots and that will not be damaged by them. Also removing large trees does not necessarily solve problems; it can often cause more structural damage than retaining them depending upon ground conditions.

Question 10: Access

If a new or improved vehicle access is required, this is a vital aspect of any scheme. It is also worth remembering that a new access from a road onto a property across a pavement will entail a pavement crossover and dropped kerb that must be constructed at the developer's expense and in full accordance with council's technical specifications.

Question 11: Fees

A fee is charged by the council for dealing with the application. It is not refunded if permission is refused or if the application is withdrawn. However, a subsequent application can be submitted with a year for free provided it is for substantially the same development on the same application site; for example the same number of houses, albeit smaller or arranged differently.

Ownership certificate

When making a planning application, it is a legal requirement that the applicant completes and signs a certificate provided with the forms, which states the ownership of the property. This is known as a section 66 certificate. If the applicant does not own the property (or bought it within the last 21 days) then the relevant notice (which must be detached from the certificate) must be served on the owner. A permission granted for an application with an incorrect certificate of ownership may be open to challenge if it can be demonstrated that the other owner of the land was seriously disadvantaged by the omission. This certificate seems to cause endless problems and is often the cause of a delay in the registering of an application. If you don't understand it, call the planning department and ask for help.

Land ownership

Land ownership is not of itself a planning issue, unless it affects the application site and area or the ability to comply with conditions. It is, however, a legal requirement that those who have an interest in an application site are informed of any application or appeal made in relation to it. To ascertain the ownership of land is supposed to be a simple matter, and it can be. The Land Registry records are searchable online for a small fee or the same information is available by filling in a form and sending it off along with the appropriate fee. To obtain the address of the relevant land registry for your area, contact the land charges section of your local council. Unregistered land can be much harder to track down and, ultimately, indemnity insurance may be required to deal with an untraceable owner or covenant holder suddenly appearing after a development had been commenced.

The plans

When the planning committee grant permission it is really just granting permission for a picture, so it follows that the more attractive the picture, the more likely you are to persuade them to grant permission. When thinking about the plans of your scheme, remember that this is all that the neighbours, the parish council and the planners have to go on. Presentation is all.

The following plans will be required, with all dimensions scaled and in metric.

1. Location plan (scale 1:1250)

This is to show the location of the site and its position in relation to the surrounding roads. This is to help the planning officer and any other interested persons to find the house. Many planning departments are able to provide copies of suitable location plans for a reasonable price

2. Site plan (scale 1:500)

This should show clearly, and accurately, the application site (marked with a red line). Marked on there should also be the position of north, the precise footprint of the proposed or existing buildings, and the position and footprint of all houses and roads directly bordering the site and all other buildings (such as garages and sheds) on the application site. Legally, what is shown outside the site is not required to be absolutely accurate as quite often site and location plans can be quite out of date. What is shown within the red line does have to be absolutely correct or the planning application and any subsequent permission may well be invalid and incapable of implementation.

3. Floor plans (scale 1:100 or 1:50)

These should show the layout of rooms of both existing and proposed parts of the existing or proposed buildings. The planning permission relates to the internal as well as the external layout.

4. Elevations (scale 1:100 or 1:50)

These are drawings of what the development will look like externally, with notation indicating what materials are to be used. It should be made clear on these drawings what is existing and what is proposed. Elevations alone can be quite misleading and are often not enough on their own to present your scheme well.

5. Street scene and perspective drawings

Money spent on showing a site in situ and presenting proposals as attractively as possible can really pay off. It helps neighbours understand what is proposed and helps the planning committee to allow it. Street scene drawings are especially useful as they enable you to show a proposed scheme in its context, illustrating the comparative scale, positioning and general appearance of a development. Without perspective drawings, or photo-real simulations, planning decisions can be overly influenced by the birds eye view shown on the site plan. This is a wholly artificial view, which is never seen and that may have very little bearing on the impact of the site on the public realm. But the site layout is potentially very important when a planning officer thinks about character of the area and density. Forcing them to imagine the three dimensional impact and what a site will actually be like once built, and how it will actually be seen, is worth doing.

The application site

This is the area of land that contains the property involved in the application. In a householder application this will simply be the whole of the garden containing the house (known in planning jargon as the 'curtilage' of the dwelling). It is important that a red line is drawn around the curtilage on the site plan because this line represents the legally binding definition of the site to which the application relates. The red line needs to be drawn on all four copies of the site plan or the application will not be registered.

Submitting the application

The application will not be registered unless it is complete and the forms correctly filled in. At this stage, call the planning department to find out when it would be convenient to have your application checked by a planning officer. Having the application checked prior to submission saves time involved in amending anything once it has been received. The application is checked for its completeness and no judgment is made as to its acceptability as a proposal. Once you have been informed that the application is registered, keep a note of the application number and find out the name of the planning officer who is dealing with it.

Revising and renewing an existing permission

You may have heard of minor amendments being allowed to existing planning permission, usually agreed by a simple exchange of letters. These changes have usually come about as people need to make minor adjustments to accommodate building regulations or errors in a site survey or just because they have changed their mind on some small issue. However, this flexibility seems to have been removed in one stroke by a recent case. The decision of Sage v Secretary of State for Environment, Transport and the Regions states "...if a building operation is not carried out, both externally and internally, fully in accordance with the permission, the whole operation is unlawful." This clearly states that the internal arrangements have to be completed in accordance with the approved plans as well as the external appearance to ensure the development is immune from enforcement action. This is a dramatic change to the flexible arrangements that used to exist. So be very careful to ensure a proposal is constructed in accordance with the approved plans.

In the event that changes are still needed, it will be necessary to make a revised application and go through the entire eight-week process again.

Renewal of permission

Until recently it was possible to renew a planning permission before it had expired by simply applying to vary a condition. This is no longer possible and any person who has not started development within the time limit allowed by the permission or consent will need to submit a fresh application. Local planning authorities will then judge such applications against current planning circumstances.

Provided that it is submitted before the expiry of the permission, this fresh application can be submitted with the minimum of detail; it is necessary only to confirm ownership of the site using the correct forms and to submit the fee and a letter requesting a renewal.

If the application has actually expired, regardless of how recently, a complete new application would be needed with all the plans etc. Whether the application is a renewal of a live permission or an application following a lapsed permission the authority are not under any legal obligation to grant the new permission, even if the old one is still live. Because the planning policies related to the site may have changed or some other material consideration may have come into play. It is particularly dangerous to assume that a longstanding and endlessly renewed permission in a protected location, such as green belt, will be granted again. Local plan policies are only getting more and more restrictive so it is a genuine possibility that old permissions will not simply be rubber stamped as they may have been in the past.

The alternative to renewal is to commence the development, so that it then lasts forever. There are reams of legal cases seeking to establish what actually constitutes lawful commencement of development, so rather than go into the small print, which is best left to lawyers, I will recommend a robust approach. The commencement of the development must be done following the clearing of all the planning conditions that require information, details or works before commencement and the work undertaken must form a genuine functioning part of the building that will result. It should be done in full accordance with the building regulations and you must be able to demonstrate that it is a genuine start to a development not just a means of seeking to prevent it expiring. The latter point is important as clearly if all you do is a minimum bit of earth moving or whatever, with no intention of carrying on, then this is arguably not actually starting the scheme at all, it is just unrelated works.

It is also worth bearing in mind that, where a planning permission incorporates separate parts of a single developmen,t once you have started one part the rest is also secured in perpetuity. For example if you have a single planning permission for a detached garage and separate extension, once you start work on one, the other is also secured. This principle was established by the case of Salisbury District Council V Secretary of State for the Environment (1982).

Chapter 9

AVOIDING A REFUSAL

It is always possible to avoid an unnecessary refusal if you keep a close eye on what is happening as your scheme works its way through the process. Once an application has been submitted you can't simply cross your fingers and wait to see what happens because you risk getting a refusal that could have been avoided. Once your application has been registered, there are a number of key dates to be aware of. The first is the end of the consultation period, which is usually three weeks following the registration date. It is during that consultation period that any previously unresolved technical problems should be picked up by the Highways Authority and other organisations who have been consulted. It is during this period that neighbours and the parish or town council will also have the opportunity to make formal representations. So when the consultation period expires, the planning officers should have all the information they need to assess the acceptability of the submitted scheme and they are legally entitled to determine the application. So the day the consultation expires you need to get in touch with the case officer immediately to find out which way the wind is blowing.

An application may be determined under delegated powers. This means that a decision can be made behind closed doors by the chief planning officer or one of his/her staff, on behalf of the elected councillors. Some local authorities have a set time each week for making delegated decisions; some make them in an ad hoc way each day. So it is very important that you understand what approach is taken to delegated decision-making by the planning department you are dealing with; they are all slightly different.

If the application is large-scale, particularly contentious, or the case officer wishes to make a recommendation contrary to the comments of the parish or town council, then it may be considered by the planning committee. Equally there are normally procedures in place to enable individual local councillors to request that a particular application is taken to committee for determination. It is an absolute priority to find out the likely recommendation of the case officer so you can try and deal with any concerns they have. Although, in many cases, this alone is not enough to predict what the eventual decision will be. It is a sad fact that many case officers will advise applicants that a proposal is acceptable in their opinion only to be overruled by their boss when it comes to the actual decision. For this reason you should always ask for the departmental recommendation, not just the case officer's own opinion.

If you discover that your application is likely be recommended for refusal, find out why and whether there is anything you can do to deal with their concerns. If they have a problem with issues of detail then a possible solution could be to withdraw the application and re-submit following agreed revisions to the plans. If their concerns are based on matters of principle then you have to make a decision. Do you withdraw the proposal and try a different kind of application or do you allow it to be refused and take it to appeal? This decision will be made on the basis of a large number of variables, including the time constraints to operating under such as the terms of the option agreement; financial considerations if the site has been bought with borrowed money; the nature of the advice you have received from a planning consultant related to the chances of success at appeal. Remember that a written representations appeal will take about six months and an informal hearing even longer.

You may wish to try and get the application taken to the planning committee in the hope that you can use some political lobbying to push forward your arguments in favour of the development. It is an important legal point that a planning decision has not been made until the decision notice has actually been issued. Different local authorities may interpret this slightly differently but in essence you are able to withdraw application at any point until the decision notice has actually been issued, which I would take to mean put in the post. So you can still withdraw application on the very night of the planning committee after they have voted to refuse it.

Because of local authority's performance indicators and customer care policies you are more likely to be stuck with a duty officer or mini call centre within the council offices than to be able to actually speak to the case officer dealing with your proposal. This means it can be very difficult to find out what's happening with your application and actually communicate with the person who may want to refuse it. To withdraw a proposal, I would recommend writing, emailing and faxing a written request to do so, keeping the evidence that this request was made.

One of the dangers of allowing the application to be refused is that the planning officers will tend to throw the book at it by adding just about any reasons for refusal they can think of so their case stands a better chance at appeal. This means that a scheme that could be negotiated, and eventually get the permission, may actually receive a completely damning refusal that can cause problems in an appeal and perhaps prevent a development that might, with some further negotiating, have been approved. As a general rule getting any planning permission, even if it is significantly less than you initially wanted, is much better than getting a refusal.

The benefit of withdrawing an application, even at the last minute, is that it keeps the slate clean in terms of planning history of the site. So even if you simply sell the land on it will retain a greater degree of hope value, therefore financial value, than if a refusal had actually been issued.

What happens if somebody objects to a proposal?

Just because someone objects does not mean that a planning application will necessarily be refused, and just because no one objects does not mean that permission will be granted. It is quite likely that the neighbours or the parish or town council may not like what you want to do regardless of its acceptability in planning terms.

Many objections to planning applications are based on envy, personal dislike and fear of property devaluation or ignorance of what is proposed. Some objections, such as concern about overlooking windows, overshadowing or loss of sunlight to windows, or concern about noise and disturbance may be well founded. It is the job of planning officers to distinguish between the two. The larger the development, the greater the prospect of objections and the government's requirement that major proposals demonstrate the involvement of local people all but guarantees an organised and articulate opposition to almost any sizeable scheme.

The consequence of objections is largely political, although I have personally noticed an increase in the instances of planning officers being influenced against a scheme apparently due to the strength of local opposition. This is not because of the planning merits of what they are saying, which in my opinion is wrong and extremely unprofessional. Objections mean that even a minor application will sometimes need to go before the planning committee for determination. The danger, in all cases when the planning officers recommend the approval of a controversial application, is that the committee may still refuse it because of sympathy for the objectors rather than because the application is genuinely harmful or unacceptable in planning terms. But because planning is so subjective they can normally find some half-reasonable planning grounds to overrule their professional advisors.

Before submitting a planning application, you are advised to talk to the neighbours about it to explain what you intend. If you can accommodate what might be fairly trivial issues, it could make the difference between a delegated approval and a committee refusal. If you do talk to the local members or parish council, think about what their real priority is - it's normally to be seen to be doing the right thing by local people. So if you design your proposal to include something you can give up, it may just tip the balance. Also be sure it's not you who is being unreasonable! Think about how you would feel in their position. If the development you want to build will overlook neighbouring windows and overshadow their gardens and stick out in the street scene like a sore thumb, then don't be surprised if other people object to it.

Parish and town councils

In some districts, particularly in rural areas, there are parish councils (in Scotland and Wales these are called community councils) and town councils. These groups of elected councillors don't have any planning powers, but they are usually consulted about planning applications and make observations on their own or their parishioners' behalf. Just because they don't object does not mean an application will be approved by the district or vice versa. As a point of interest many such councillors are not elected, they simply stand unopposed. The district councils do take note of what parish or town councils have to say. If they object, an application will usually need to go before the planning committee in the same way as if a neighbour were to object. Therefore, it is often worth attempting to forestall such objections by talking to the parish councillors about what you wish to do and what their priorities are.

Borough/district councillors - your representatives

Many elected councillors are terrified of getting involved in planning controversies because it is hard not to upset at least one half of the protagonists. There is also a lot of anxiety about probity and the concern not to be seen to favour either side. Councils have different policies on this issue, some are extremely paranoid and try and prevent virtually any contact between developers and councillors, or even the public and councillors on planning issues. It is ironic that the ward councilor for any development site is often so hamstrung by concerns about probity that they can hardly make any representations on behalf of the people who elected them. Or take a view on commercial interests that create employment, or whatever, without becoming venerable to accusations of bias and corruption. So do not be surprised if, when seeking to talk to local councillors about a proposed development, you get a frosty reception.

Notwithstanding the above, two things are still worth remembering:
1. It is the elected councillors on the planning committees, or planning officers acting on their behalf, who make the decisions on planning applications.

2. The planning officers make decisions only on behalf of the councillors. The councillors are elected representatives and they, in effect, have to reapply for their jobs every four or so years.

This knowledge may help in a number of ways

■ If you know that neighbours objects strongly to your proposal and have been lobbying the members of the planning committee, it may be worth contacting and presenting information to the local councilor, particularly if he or she is a also a member of the planning committee. Be careful not to be too pushy because too much pestering and lobbying may end up being counterproductive. More oblique pressure can be more effective.

■ If you are advised that your application is to be refused under delegated authority it may be worth requesting that it is considered by the committee. Persuading them to make a committee site visit could also ensure that your proposal gets a fair and full consideration.

■ If the neighbours raise strong objections to what you wish to do, they may persuade the councillors to refuse your application against the advice of the planning officers. In these circumstances (time permitting) it could be well worth appealing against a refusal but bear in mind that a win is still not guaranteed.

Chapter 10
PLANNING APPEALS

Despite your best efforts, sometimes applications are refused. This section outlines the most common reasons for refusal of minor domestic proposals and what areas can be appealed against successfully. The reasons for refusal of substantial developments are more llikely to be policy based and beyond the scope of this book; bearing in mind the number of potential local development plan policies that could be involved.

Reasons for refusal in small-scale domestic applications

■ Conflict with character of existing dwelling. The proposed extension due to its design, bulk and siting fails to harmonise with the scale and character of the existing dwelling. The extension will appear as an intrusive or incongruous feature to the substantial detriment of the character and amenities of the area.

■ Overlooking. The proposed development is poorly sited in that it would overlook and be overlooked by existing neighbouring property. Permission for such a development would have a detrimental effect on the character and amenities of that neighbouring property and the character and amenities of the development itself would be detrimentally affected by the neighbouring property.

■ Overshadowing. The scale, bulk and height of the proposed extension

is excessive and would have an overshadowing and overbearing effect on neighbouring properties.

■ Reduction of existing rear garden. The proposal would result in an unacceptable reduction in the size of the existing rear garden, which would consequently be inadequate to serve the existing house.

■ Insufficient detail. This application cannot be considered acceptable without further details indicating the effects of the proposed development on the surrounding area and, despite a written request, these details have not been submitted.

All these reasons involve quite a hefty degree of subjective opinion and depend upon a reasonable interpretation of the phrases used.

Who can appeal?

The only person who can appeal against a refusal of permission is the person who made the planning application. There is no right of appeal by objectors to an application who feel that it should not have been permitted, nor can an appeal be made by someone in support of a planning application that has been refused. The right to appeal against a condition that is attached to a planning permission is not limited to the original applicant, which makes sense as a site may change hands before the problem with a condition is established.

What can be appealed against?

You may appeal if:

■ You do not accept a condition, which has been attached to a planning permission and wish to have it removed or its terms varied.

■ The local authority does not decide your application within eight weeks. This needs to be considered in the context of the time it takes for the

planning inspectorate to determine the appeal. This eight-week period appeal is usually used by people who, knowing they will be refused, wish to lodge an appeal as soon as possible (while perhaps negotiating on a duplicate application.

Find out exactly what the problems are by talking directly to the planning officer involved. The reasons for refusal on the decision notice can sometimes be ambiguous and hard to follow. If you did not submit the proposal following consultations, find out if changes to the plans in a new application would overcome the reasons for refusal.

Find out from the planning department whether the planning committee considered your application. If so, was it recommended for approval by the planning officers? If the committee overturned the advice of the planning officers, then it may be that the issues were finely balanced or that the application was not refused for sound planning reasons. In this situation it is often worth appealing.

It is very difficult to talk in general terms about what is more or less likely to gain approval at appeal. The best guide is to consider what you applied for against the polices and supplementary guidance that have been adopted by the local authority. If you live in an area that is designated as a conservation area, national park or area of outstanding natural beauty then the controls on the quality of materials, design, and emphasis on traditional local building styles will be greater. If you live in a normal, residential area, then a refusal based purely on judgments about unattractive design could be worth appealing against if you have evidence from a qualified architect to support your case.

If you do decide to appeal you must do so within six months of the refusal.

Should you Appeal?

The reason it is so important to avoid a refusal is that it places a black mark on the planning history of the plot and establishes very clearly what isn't

acceptable. It is also a fact of life that planning authorities will often throw every reason for refusal they can think of in an attempt to ensure they win any appeal. Thereafter, anything you apply for will be compared to the refused scheme. If you decide to appeal to the independent planning inspectorate they can take up to a year to come to a decision.

If you have had a refusal on the basis of a basic principle of planning policies do stop and think very carefully about how realistic you're being. If you get a refusal on an issue of detail and you can wait a year it might be worth appealing if you have an arguable case. Otherwise, I would normally recommend not going to appeal as it is very risky and the comments of an appeal inspector will be given great importance by the local authority. If he dismisses the appeal, this can destroy any development potential a site might have for many years. Make sure you only appeal when you really have no other choice.

Cost and time

These are the two most influential factors in reaching the decision to go to appeal.

■ Cost: There is no fee to pay when making an appeal. The only costs are those resulting from paying for planning advice or representation, or the effort you may put in yourself. You do not need to employ a professional planning consultant to lodge an appeal but it will almost certainly be more effective if you do. Even if you are clear about the arguments for and against your proposal, and you feel confident, you are unlikely to be able to make a reasonable case without the help of a planning consultant unless it is a very small-scale domestic application.

■ Time: This is often the planning officer's greatest bargaining point, although he or she is unlikely to admit this. Making an appeal is likely to take at least six months from start to finish and could take up to a year. The type of appeal you choose will influence the length of time taken before a decision will be made

Who decides the outcome of a planning appeal?

Planning Appeals are decided by an inspector appointed by and acting on behalf of the Government.

What sort of appeal should you make?

There are three sorts of appeal process:

- Written representations
- Informal hearings
- Public inquiries

Written representations

This is usually the simplest and quickest method of appeal.

■ A written statement is submitted stating why you feel that you have a case (why permission should have been granted.

■ The local authority will produce a written statement putting forward their case in support of their reasons for refusal.

■ You then exchange statements and each has an opportunity to comment on the other side's view.

■ A planning inspector receives both statements, plus any additional factual background information and letters of objection or support from neighbouring residents or other interested parties.

■ He or she will then make a site visit.

■ You will be informed of the date and time of the site visit so that you can be present, but no discussion of the case is permitted on site.

■ After lengthy consideration, about five weeks, the inspector sends both parties the decision by letter.

■ Any interested party may request from the inspector that he/she is sent a copy of the other party's statement to comment on (but in practice these are usually submitted at the same time at the end of the six week period).

Informal hearings

■ The hearing consists of a meeting between the appellant (with or without an agent or planning consultant, highway engineer and any other relevant professionals who can give evidence), a representative of the local planning department, a planning inspector and any other interested third parties such as the parish council.

■ The pros and cons of the proposal will then be discussed. In this method, written statements are exchanged before the hearing, but you are entitled to see the local authority's statement before you submit your own.

■ A site visit will be made, and the inspector may continue discussions there.

■ The inspector will then consider what he/she has heard and inform both parties by letter of his or her decision within about five weeks of the end of the hearing.

Public inquiries

■ The public inquiry procedure is very formal and can be quite intimidating to the uninitiated. It is usual for both sides to be represented by solicitors, barristers or other advocates.

■ Before the exchange of statements of case, both sides must agree a statement of common ground in an attempt to limit the focus of the debate in the inquiry to the key issues rather than wasting time on peripheral matters over which there is little disagreement.

■ Statements of case are read by planning witnesses and each side has the opportunity of cross-examining the other and of making a final verbal summing up.

■ Public inquiries are usually reserved for significant development proposals or complicated cases involving unauthorised developments. They are confrontational, long-winded and expensive. I have heard it said that the chances of winning an appeal are higher via an inquiry, but I have not seen any real evidence to support this.

Which sort of appeal is best?

The choice for the householder, builder or developer, who is involved in small-scale proposals, is between written representation or informal hearings. Written representations are the fastest route although in my opinion the informal hearing provides a better and more effective opportunity to really explain the case and for the local authority to have to try and justify reasons for refusal. It is reassuring to note that planning inspectors are trained to take account of the difficulties faced by householders attempting to justify their proposals against experienced planners. This being the case, an informal hearing may often be worth trying if time is not of the essence. Anyone may be present at such a hearing including supporters and objectors to your scheme.

Claims for costs

Costs cannot be claimed against the other side in a written representation appeal, so informal hearings are often chosen with this in mind. Costs can be sought if the reasons for refusal have not been substantiated by evidence or if either party has behaved unreasonably, either in refusing an application that should have been allowed or in appealing against a refusal in circumstances where there was no reasonable prospect of success. The issue of costs is dealt with by Government Circular 05/00: Planning Appeals Procedures, which can be found on the Communities and Local Government website.

What do you say?

Arguments in favour of your proposal should be confined to those aspects which are relevant to planning. These are called material considerations.

The following factors are not generally considered 'material' to the determination of an appeal, so there is no point in putting these forward in your case.

■ The property would be more valuable if the planning permission was granted.

■ The proposal would improve your view.

■ You need the extra space.

■ There has been a lot of development in the area recently anyway.

■ Your intentions are not based on financial gain.

■ You have been able to get a cheap deal on the design and materials proposed.

■ You are a local person.

Factors which are more likely to be material and which could be worth mentioning are:

■ The harmless effect of the proposal on the residential amenities of neighbouring houses, in terms of privacy sunlight and daylight aspect.

■ The effect of the proposal in terms of its appearance and the visual amenities of its surroundings.

Arguments in favour of the look of the proposal may include:

■ The proposal is in keeping with its surroundings. Either because the

design and siting and general scale reflect those elements found in other buildings in the area, or the surroundings have no special or discernible character or particular features with which it is necessary or desirable to conform.

■ The local authority has not identified the area, which includes the application site, as having any special character or significance, or as containing any special features worthy of preservation. Therefore, a refusal in terms of design alone is unjustified.

■ The proposal is similar in appearance to other developments permitted elsewhere in the vicinity.

■ Entirely suitable materials are being proposed for use in the development if it is approved.

■ No trees are being affected; new trees and shrubs will be planted.

More general arguments could include:

■ The views from neighbouring properties are not inviolate; there is no right to a certain view.

■ The application should be considered on its merits and only be refused if there is conflict with the development plan and demonstrable harm (planning jargon for a very good reason).

Although an application may not conform to some elements of the development plan, other material considerations may still indicate that it should be approved.

■ Planning policies. It will be worth analysing the relevant local development plan or local development framework for any arguments which would support your case, or indications that you should negotiate, or that you may as well give up and abandon the proposal altogether.

Local plans/Local development frameworks

A local plan, or now re-branded local development framework, is a document that contains planning policies for the area covered by a particular local planning authority. It is produced after a long process of public consultation and is agreed by the Department of the Environment. Such plans tend to be revised every five years. The policies contained in them tend to be most influential when the plan is up to date and has been formally adopted by the council concerned. The older a local plan is the less weight an appeal inspector will give it when balancing the pros and cons of a proposal. Local plans often contain policies that are relevant to small-scale private developments such as house extensions.

Will the planning department help you to appeal?

You have the right to see public documents relating to your application and details of other planning permissions etc held by your local planning department. Before appealing it would be worth investigating the history of planning decisions related to your house, and perhaps similar proposals in the area. Odd though it sounds, the planning department still has the job of assisting you, even if it is to appeal against their refusal. So don't be afraid to seek the advice of planning officers when making an appeal, even if you know they do not support your proposal.

Government advice

There is a bewildering mass of government advice contained primarily in Planning Policy Guidance Notes and Planning Policy Statements and Circulars issued by what is currently called the Department of Communities and Local Government. These cover the whole range of planning issues and are updated on a frighteningly regular basis. This government advice is important and one of the key influences which the inspector will weigh up when deciding the merits of a particular case. They can all be found on the Communities and Local Government website www.communities.gov.uk and on The Planning Portal website.

The most important current government advice is PPS 3 Housing. (For future updates on policy issues visit www.housebuildersupdate.co.uk) Any inspector is likely to be very familiar with current government advice but it will do no harm to remind him or her of it because it will almost certainly be more up to date and, therefore, more important than the council's own policies.

The majority of small homeowner planning applications will not be determined one way or another as a result of specific national planning policies but rather due to other detail arguments. But for larger applications such policies can be crucial.

What if you lose the appeal?

The inspector's decision letter will clearly set out the reasons for the decision. It may be that you can overcome these problems by changes to your proposal. In that case, submit a new application accordingly.

You can only challenge the decision on a point of law, or if you feel that the requirements of planning legislation or procedures have been ignored. You cannot challenge it simply because you disagree with the decision. Any challenge has to be made through the high court, and expensive legal advice will be needed. My advice is to forget it.

The Ombudsman

IIf you feel strongly that you have been seriously disadvantaged because the planning authority has not followed the correct procedure in dealing with an application, then you can make a complaint to the ombudsman. You can complain if you are the applicant, neighbour, or anyone else. However, it is very important to understand that the ombudsman is not interested in the professional judgement of the planners; he or she is there purely to police the correct implementation of administrative procedures. Also, if you think certain procedures should have been carried out, make sure that you thoroughly understand what should have been done and

10

be clear about exactly what omission you object to and why.

More information regarding the work of the Ombudsman may be obtained from www.lgo.org.uk or by post from:
The Secretary
Commission for Local Administration in England
21 Queen Anne's Gate
London
SW1H9BU

Even if the Ombudsman finds mal-administration, they may decide there was actually no prejudice to you and even if they think there was, the amount of compensation they tend to recommend is paltry and, finally, it is in any event only advisory. The Ombudsman has no teeth. A local authority might be embarrassed and be morally obliged to cough up a few hundred quid but little more. So before becoming obsessed and wasting months pursuing a possibly entirely well-justified vendetta against your local authority, please remember that it is probably a complete waste of your time and you would be better off putting it down to experience and moving on. Life is, generally, too short.

Chapter 11
BUILDING REGULATIONS

Building regulations approval is an entirely separate requirement to planning permission with different legislation and different processes. This brief chapter is included because once planning permission is obtained you will usually need to get building regulations approval. However, there is a range of building works which require building regulations approval but not planning permission, and vice versa. Sometimes you don't need either.

What work requires building regulation approval?

Building Regulations approval is required if you intend to carry out any of the following works:

■ Erect a new building or extend an existing building (unless it is covered by the list of exemptions below and later).

■ Make structural alterations to a building, including underpinning.

■ Alter the number of dwellings within a building

■ In certain cases, a change of use.

■ Provide, extend or alter drainage facilities.

■ Install a heat producing appliance (with the exception of gas appliances installed by persons approved under the Gas Safety regulations).

■ Install cavity insulation.

■ Install an unvented hot water storage system.

■ Electrical works to domestic premises

■ Electrical works to domestic premises

■ Renovate a thermal element i.e. re-render an external, totally replace a floor, wall or re-roof a property. In these cases, you will be required to insulate that element to current standards.

■ Carry out works which will affect the means of escape in case of fire

When is approval not required?

You do not need Building Regulations approval to:

■ Carry out certain very minor works to electric wiring unless they are in a kitchen, bathroom or outside.

■ Install new sanitaryware, so long as it doesn't involve new drainage or plumbing arrangements.

■ Carry out repairs as long as they are of a minor nature and replace like for like.

It's as well to contact the Building Control department if you're in any doubt about whether or not you need to apply for Building Regulations approval.

In addition to the exclusions listed above there are common types of building work that are exempt from the regulations:

■ The erection of a detached single storey building with a floor area of less than 30 square metres, so long as it does not contain any sleeping accommodation, no part of it is less than one metre from any boundary and it is constructed of non combustible material.

■ The erection of any detached building not exceeding 15 square metres, so long as there is no sleeping accommodation.

■ The extension of a building by a ground floor extension of a) a conservatory, porch, covered yard or covered way, or, b) a carport open on a least two sides, so long as, in any of those cases, the floor area of the extension does not exceed 30 square metres. In the case of a conservatory or a wholly or partially glazed porch, the glazing has to satisfy the requirements of those parts of the Building Regulations dealing with glazing materials and protection.

To qualify as a porch, the structure must envelope an existing external door which must remain in place. A conservatory must be unheated and separated form the dwelling by doors

Making an application to the Local Authority

It is worth noting that in England and Wales you may choose to submit an Initial Notice via an Approved Inspector. When seeking approval from your local council there are two alternative methods which you can use:

A Full Plans Application

In this method you or your agent submits to the council duplicate application forms with two full sets of drawings (four sets for a commercial building) of the work you propose. These drawings must be sufficiently detailed to enable the council to determine whether the work will comply with the relevant regulations, and should include:

■ A site plan at a scale of 1:1250 clearly showing the proposed building or extension and with a clear indication of the boundaries of the property

■ Plans, sections and elevations as necessary to a scale of 1:50 or 1:100

■ Detailed specifications of all materials and methods of construction used and fire precautions

■ Appropriate calculations of thermal insulation and structural elements where reliance is not placed on the information contained in the approved documents attached to the regulations

If the information submitted is deficient or inadequate it will delay the application and may result in a rejection of the plans. However, most councils will contact you to seek clarification of what you propose, or amendments, when this would lead to an approval. You do not have to wait until you receive approval to start work although all work is at your own risk if you do start prematurely – planning ahead is always worthwhile.

Increasingly you may be able to submit your application electronically either using an internet based resource or simply by emailing the plans and completed forms. Your local Building Control section will have more information on this and many other issues on its website, as well as downloadable forms, guidance notes and charges schedules.

When such an application is approved you or your agent receives:

■ A notice of approval which may have conditions attached
■ A set of drawings stamped as approved
■ Printed inspection request cards are not normally provided any more as inspections can be booked over the telephone, by email or even by sms text message in some instances

These documents are usually necessary should you be seeking finance to assist in the extension or building work from a bank or building society and are essential as part of the Home Information Pack on sale of the house to show that the necessary approvals were obtained. The approval notice and approved plans are important documents; they cannot normally be replaced, and should be kept safely, as should all written correspondence from the council.

The building notice procedure

This method is somewhat easier and simpler, initially, than the deposit of full plans. You or your agent simply make a written application on the appropriate form and may start work straight away. Full plans are not required, although a 1:1250 block plan with boundaries and any new buildings or extensions clearly marked is required to help check for public sewers and for fire brigade access in the case of a new dwelling.

The control of building work is exercised by site inspection at the necessary stages. Generally, more inspections are required if you choose to use this route, as the assumption is that you or your builder have full knowledge of all regulations and technical standards and can therefore work without plans.

You are advised to check whether this is the case, particularly when accepting an estimate without a detailed Building Regulation drawing or specification. The object of the building control officer in making inspections is not to supervise the operation or act as a Clerk of Works. They cannot act as a design consultant or surveyor on your behalf. There are disadvantages to such a method and you should carefully consider them before embarking upon building work by building notice.

On receipt of a valid notice in this form your local council will respond with:

■ A document accepting the building notice

■ You do not receive written approval of your proposals so this route may not satisfy your lender

During the progress of the work you may be asked to provide details and calculations of particular elements of your work, but you will not be asked for full plans. Plans requested in this case must be necessary for the council to determine compliance and will be requested in writing.

Generally speaking I would only advise using this method for very small-

scale building works. If work to be approved under the notice system is sub-standard, then it will have to be taken down and re-built at your own cost. Where the work involves building over a public sewer then it would be foolhardy to proceed without the security of a full plans approval, as the water authority can require that the building or extension be removed.

You cannot use the Building Notice procedure for:
■ Commercial buildings
■ Flats where there are common areas
■ New dwellings located in private roads
■ Buildings or extensions which affect or are affected by a public sewer

If you have already carried out work and now realise that you should have made an application, you can apply for a Regularisation Certificate, providing the work was carried out after October 1985. You will have to supply details, plans and possibly calculations to show what was done and also expose elements of the building to show whether it complied with the requirements in force at the time. A charge is payable for this service.

Building regulation fees and charges

Building regulation charges are set by government statute although they vary considerably as all Local Authority Building Control bodies are required to cover their own costs, which also vary. These are sometimes payable in two stages. A plans fee must be paid on deposit of full plans, and is intended to cover the costs of the council in processing and approving the application.

A further charge (which is known as the inspection charge) is usually payable once the work starts on site although for smaller projects these charges are usually combined.

Details of the levels of charges are available from your local Building Control provider – you may be able to pay over the telephone using a debit card or using a secure web site.

The combined charge is the same whichever route you choose to follow.

Do neighbours have the right to object?

No. However, it is always advisable to be neighbourly and to tell them what you are doing. You may find that it could help to have access from their land in the future. Remember that you should not build on or over their land without their formal written consent.

You should also be a ware of the requirements of the Party Wall Act. This is not enforced by a Local Authority as it is a civil matter. You must serve notice on your neighbours if work will affect a party wall or boundary or be within 3m of one. Each side can appoint a Party Wall surveyor at the expense of the person having the work carried out to ensure that a schedule is drawn up and agreed before work commences. The RICS can advise you on finding a Party Wall surveyor.

What happens if your work does not comply?

The local authority can serve a notice on you to alter or remove it. If you refuse to comply, the Local Authority will carry out any necessary urgent works themselves and recover their costs from you, and will take legal action through the Magistrates Court.

Are there penalties for contravening building regulations?

Yes. If you build without notifying the local authority, or carry out work which does not comply then you are liable to be fined. The penalty may be up to £2000, plus £50 for each day the contravention continues after conviction. However, once a building is fully completed for 12 months or more a local authority cannot prosecute you although they will record the contraventions on the Land Charges Register and you will find it very difficult to sell or let the property until the work is rectified.

In cases affecting safety, the Council can seek an injunction and have the work put right at your expense.

The Building Regulations documents

In **England and Wales** the various sections of the Building Regulations are:

Approved Document A – Structure

Approved Document B - Fire safety

Approved Document C - Site preparation and resistance to contamination and moisture

Approved Document D - Toxic substances

Approved Document E - Resistance to the passage of sound

Approved Document F – Ventilation

Approved Document G – Hygiene

Approved Document H - Drainage and waste disposal

Approved Document J - Combustion appliances and fuel storage systems

Approved Document K - Protection from falling, collision and impact

Approved Document L1 - Conservation of fuel and power

Approved Document M - Access and facilities for disabled people

Approved Document N - Glazing. Safety relating to impact, opening & cleaning

Approved Document P – Electrical safety

There is also an Approved Document to support Regulation 7 – materials & workmanship.

In **Scotland** the Building Standards documents are:

Section 0 - General – Introduction, exemptions, changes of use, durability and workmanship, building standards and security of buildings.

Section 1 - Structure

Section 2 - Fire

Section 3 - Environment

Section 4 - Safety

Section 5 - Noise

Section 6 - Energy

Appendix 'A' defines the terms.

Appendix 'B' lists the standards and other publications.

Appendix 'C' cross references the new numbered regulations to the old lettered ones.

You can access a fully searchable version of these standards and document on the Planning Portal website http://www.planningportal.gov.uk

Chapter 12
UNAUTHORISED DEVELOPMENT

Many people are unclear about the requirements of planning permission and, despite having the best of intentions, they can find themselves at odds with the local planning department. This can occur because of simple ignorance, incorrect advice or a lack of communication between the different parties involved in a development. If you are in this position, don't panic. Planning authorities frequently have to deal with such occurrences and if the situation is approached the right way, it can usually be resolved amicably and without drama.

Enforcement

Enforcement is a local authority's term for the set of procedures used to enforce planning laws. Planning departments usually have enforcement officers who spend their time following up complaints about unauthorised developments. The legal procedures and ins and outs of the enforcement system are complicated and beyond the scope of this guide, but a summary is outlined below to help those who have become involved. This includes those people who believe that others seem to have 'got away with it'.

The four and ten-year rules

If something has been built without permission, and has stood for four

years with no action taken by the planning authority during that time, then the unauthorised building becomes immune from enforcement. This is known as the four-year rule. The logic behind this is that if something can go unnoticed for four years it can't be much of a problem, so it effectively gets permission. The four-year rule also applies to the change of use of any building into a private dwelling, whether or not in breach of an occupancy condition, but not to other changes of use, which fall under the ten-year rule.

The ten-year rule applies to other non-residential changes of use, which, if unchallenged for ten or more years, become immune from any action. Conditions attached to a planning permission, other than those related to residential occupancy, also fall within the ten-year limit. If they have not been complied with for ten years, then in most cases they cannot be enforced.

Will enforcement action always be taken?

There are three situations in which enforcement may be taken:

■ When something has been built, or an activity is occurring, which requires, but does not have, planning permission and the local authority are firmly of the view that it would not be granted.

■ When planning permission has been granted for a building but it is not being (or has not been) built in accordance with the plans submitted, both internally and externally.

■ When permission has been granted subject to conditions but these have been ignored and are being breached.

The following procedures are likely to be adopted by the enforcement officer in dealing with the first two possibilities..

Negotiation and request for retrospective application

An enforcement officer working with the planning department will investigate the breach and make a visit to the property involved. If it is considered that what has occurred is likely to be acceptable, or made acceptable through minor changes, then negotiations may be attempted. As part of these negotiations, a retrospective planning application may be requested. A time limit is likely to be given by the planning authority to the person responsible to either rectify the breach or make an application.

Certificates of lawful use or development

There is a procedure for obtaining a certificate of lawful use or development (LDC) from your local planning department. This constitutes a formal and legally binding decision by the local authority that a particular proposed or existing use or development does not require planning permission and is lawful. Its effects are similar to a planning permission and conditions may be attached. If you need legally binding evidence then a LDC is necessary.

There was a period when a LDC was likely to be required only in special circumstances, for example where an applicant and the local authority were in dispute. However, this is no longer the case as it is now the only way to formally establish whether planning permission is required for a proposed development or whether an existing development or use is lawful. If you become involved in applying for a LDC, I recommend that you employ a fully qualified planning consultant. (For more information see Circular 10/97: Enforcing planning control: legislative provisions and procedural requirements and Section 10 of the Planning and Compensation Act 1991).

Requests for further information

Legal steps can be taken to find out more about the breach of control:

■ Requisition for information notice: This is served in order to establish who has a legal interest in the property involved.

■ Planning contravention notice: In addition to the above questions, this notice can ask for specific and detailed information about the nature of the breach.

In both cases, failure to complete and return the relevant forms, or the giving of false information, can result in the prosecution of the person responsible. Receipt of one of these indicates that things are getting serious.

Enforcement notice

This is the main tool used by planning authorities against unauthorised developments and other breaches of planning control. The enforcement notice is a legal document served on the person involved in breach of planning control if:

■ A retrospective planning application is not submitted.

■ A retrospective application is submitted but is subsequently refused.

■ The breach is considered unacceptable and undesirable irrespective of the submission of an application.

The enforcement notice outlines the nature of the breach of planning control and the steps required to rectify it and why it should be rectified. The notice will take effect a minimum of one month after it is served. If an appeal is not lodged at least one month after it takes effect, then the person involved may be prosecuted and fined on a regular basis until the breach has been rectified.

Appealing against an enforcement notice

An appeal against an enforcement notice may be made to the Department

of the Environment within one month of the notice taking effect. The appeal will follow basically the same course as a normal planning appeal. If the appellant wins the appeal then they have got planning permission (this may be subject to conditions). If the appeal is lost and the breach is not rectified during the time given by the appeal inspector, then prosecution can take place. Implicit within an enforcement appeal is consideration of granting planning permission for the development involved as if the appeal was against a refusal of permission.

Stop notices

A stop notice is available, which can be served immediately following an enforcement notice. This may be required when some unauthorised activity is taking place which is harmful (ongoing building works or unpleasant industrial activities, for instance). The stop notice means that whatever is going on must cease, or prosecution will result immediately. These notices are not served often because if it transpires that the notice was legally incorrect, then the local planning authority fears it could be liable to pay compensation for any lost income resulting from the notice. This is rarely the case but because they are used so infrequently there is a lack of confidence in their use, despite the availability of the temporary stop notice that is legally less onerous for the council. Despite the theoretical ease of use of these temporary notices local authorities are still very reluctant to use them.

Enforcement of conditions

In the event of people failing to implement planning conditions, the local authority may take immediate and effective action.

For example, if one of the conditions of your permission notice is that a certain window must be obscure glazed (to prevent overlooking) and this has not been done, a breach of condition notice may be served on you that will demand that obscured glazing is fitted. A minimum of 28 days will be given by the notice for the work to be carried out. If this is not done, magistrates may impose a fine for every day until the condition has been complied with. The only defence in court against prosecution is that the person charged took all reasonable measures to carry out what is required by the notice.

This is a speedy and effective means of enforcement, which could prove expensive for the person charged and give them a criminal record. Conditions may be appealed against at any time but you risk prosecution by carrying out a development without complying, whether an appeal has been lodged or not.

Amended plans & letters of comfort - no longer an option

There was a time when, if a planning officer wrote you a letter, for example declaring that you did or did not need planning permission or that the provisions of a particular planning condition could be ignored or that something was now immune from enforcement action, that you had some reasonable grounds to give that letter some legal weight. It was believed that a senior officer of a council to bind the hands of that authority in a way that would stop it taking any contrary action. This has the legal term of 'estoppel' and it was assumed that letters, even phone calls, could 'estop' the local authority from contradicting a previously expressed view or opinion.

In 2003 all this changed. But it is surprising how many people, including planners, are still unaware of it. The decision of the House of Lords in R v. E Sussex CC (ex p Reprotech) in 2003 established beyond all doubt that there is NO scope for the doctrine of estoppel in planning law. So the helpful assurances of a planning officer cannot, in any way, bind the Council. The logic here is that if there is a formal mechanism available – such as an application to relax a planning condition or an application for a Lawful Development Certificate to establish whether planning permission is needed or not – then a letter, however carefully or strongly worded, is no substitute for that correct legal procedure under the Planning Acts.

This is, of course, a pain in the derrière as it means that you cannot seek real legal comfort without becoming involved in bureaucracy. In practice people still write to local authorities to ask if they need consent and to clarify other issues. It is all very informal but it helps homeowners to move forward, sell their houses and make decisions. Do be careful and remember that legally, letter or no letter, you're on your own!

Incidentally, other forms of planning advice provided by officers at the pre-application stage, and even during the consideration of a proposal, have even less weight!

Conclusion - the right attitude

As a general rule local planning authorities do not have the manpower to check that all new buildings that are built have planning permission, or that they are built in exact accordance with the internal and external layouts and designs of the plans granted planning permission. Therefore, enforcement action is likely to be the result of complaints from neighbours or the eagle eyed vigilance of the zealous members of local parish or town councils who seem to have lots of time on their hands. Small minded, interfering busybodies is a rather emotive phrase that I have heard used in relation to some of them. Certainly there can be a significant lack of 'live and let live' in the attitudes of local elected representatives.

Planning authorities do not generally go around looking for trouble and they are advised by central government to seek compromise in dealing with unauthorised development. On the other hand, the planning system exists to control and restrict development and people do not like seeing it ignored, especially if they objected to a development in the first place.

So, whatever the problem encountered, taking the right attitude will help. Whether you are an objector, or someone who has built something without permission, talking to the planners in a civil and helpful manner is more likely to achieve what you want than being difficult or confrontational.

Note: unauthorised works to listed buildings do not benefit from the four-year-rule and are not considered in this chapter. They may be dealt with by immediate prosecution and potentially severe criminal penalties (see Appendix II).

Appendix I
PERMITTED DEVELOPMENT

The government is currently reviewing all domestic permitted development rights and the allowances set out here may change. Please visit www.housebuildersupdate.co.uk to check for updates as they happen. The details of permitted development rights set out here generally applies to England and Wales; the situation in Scotland is dealt with in a separate section at the end of this chapter.

Permitted development is a term used to describe things that a homeowner can construct without the need to make a planning application. This is a potentially confusing subject, but if it is approached methodically it will become clear that a lot can be done without the need to obtain planning permission.

Permitted development rights apply to the majority of houses and they are, in effect, a general permission granted by central government for a wide range of minor works. These rights do not apply to flats other than with regard to the erection of a limited number of satellite dishes.

Permitted development rights are not the same countrywide and are occasionally modified by local planning authorities. In the first instance it is useful to establish whether your house still has the benefit of the full range of these rights. The following factors need to be considered.

Designated areas

What is allowed as permitted development is more restricted within the areas of:

- National parks
- Areas of outstanding natural beauty
- Conservation areas
- The Norfolk and Suffolk broads

Planning conditions

In some situations, typically on high-density housing estates, the planning permission granted for the houses will contain a condition removing all or some of the permitted development rights. For instance, on some estates the right to enclose front gardens by one-metre high fences is removed so that the estates remain open plan. Where houses have integral garages, the right to convert these garages into rooms is sometimes removed, to ensure that future parking provision is adequate.

Article Four directions

A local authority can remove or reduce permitted development rights by serving an article four direction. This will remain in force for six months during which it must be confirmed by the government. Once confirmed, the direction becomes permanent. The local authority must give justification for this direction and anyone whose property is affected can appeal. If planning permission is refused for a development, which would have had permitted development had it not been for an Article Four direction, then compensation is payable for the loss in property value incurred.

Previous extensions

Permitted development rights do enable houses to be extended a certain amount before planning permission is required. Once the maximum has been reached, all further additions require permission. This means that if your house has been extended in the past, your right to extend may have been partially or entirely used up. If an extension is so large that it exceeds the maximum allowed as permitted development, and it is granted planning permission and built, all further extensions will require permission.

Useful definitions

Before explaining the details of what may be done without permission a small number of phrases need to be explained. These phrases will not make much sense until you attempt to understand how the permitted development regulations relate to your own property.

The original house

This refers to the house as it was first built prior to any additions. If a house was built prior to July 1 1948, the definition of original house is as the house stood on that date. Some planning inspectors have accepted the demolition of existing parts of a house and their reconstruction without leading to the loss of permitted development rights provided what has been demolished and rebuilt was part of the original house.

Extensions

■ This does include conservatories. In permitted development terms a conservatory is treated as an extension.

■ Any outbuildings built in your garden since the house was built, which are located within five metres of any part of the house, will count against the permitted development allowance for extensions. So in effect they are treated as an extension.

■ Any extension to the original house, which would come within five metres of any existing outbuilding, will cause that outbuilding to be treated as an extension in terms of the permitted development allowance.

■ Where outbuildings (including garages) were built at the same time as the original house, and are closer to it than five metres, they will be considered as part of the original house for the purposes of calculating the amount of permitted development available.

■ All outbuildings in conservation areas, which are more than ten cubic metres in size and which were built after the original house, are treated as if they are extensions to the house and count against the permitted development allowance.

Volume

Measurements of volume are used extensively in describing the amount which can be built as permitted development. All such measurements are based on external dimensions and it includes the roof.

Height

Where measurements of height are used in relation to buildings, it is assumed that the measurement is taken from ground level immediately adjacent to the building that is being erected. If the levels vary, the measurement is taken from the highest part of the ground. In the case of walls and fences, if ground levels vary then the measurement is taken from the surrounding 'natural' ground level.

Highway

When used in relation to walls and fences this only refers to roads, which carry vehicular traffic but it includes the width of the footpath or verges on either side. So when distances are measured from the highway they will usually be taken from the property boundary next to the road. When used in relation to distances from the house itself or extensions to the house, the term 'highway' includes footpaths, not just roads that carry vehicles. In both cases, the term refers to any highway which runs along any boundary of the house, not just at the front.

I want to build an extension: how do PD rights affect me?

You will not require planning permission to extend your house provided that you comply with the following.

■ Position: No extension should be built closer to any highway than any part of the existing house, unless the distance between the extension and the highway is 20m or more. No more than half of the area of land around the original house should be covered by extensions (or other additional buildings).

■ Size: In the case of a terraced (or end terrace) house the maximum size of extension is ten per cent of the volume of the original house or up to 50 cubic metres, whichever is the greater. For other kinds of houses, including the maximum allowed, is 15 per cent of the volume of the original house or up to 70 cubic metres, whichever is the greater. In any case the maximum should not exceed a total of 115 cubic metres.

■ Height: If the extension is within two metres of the boundary of the property, it must not exceed four metres in height. If the extension is two metres or more from the boundary then it must not be higher than the highest part of the roof of the original house.

Roof extensions

Planning permission is required for any additions or extensions to the roof of a house. You will not require planning permission provided that you comply with the following:

■ Position: No additions or extensions are allowed on any roof slope which faces a highway.

■ Size: The maximum size that may be added to the roof of a terraced (or end terrace) house is 40 cubic metres. For other kinds of houses, including bungalows, the maximum permitted is 50 cubic metres. These quantities are permitted as part of, and not in addition to, the maximum amount available for extensions.

■ Height: No roof extension should be higher than the highest part of the original house (excluding chimneys).

Roof lights/sky lights

Planning permission is not required for roof lights on any roof slope.

Solar panels and wind turbines

The installation of solar panels is acceptable provided that they do not project significantly beyond the roof slope. It is anticipated that the government will make small-scale energy generating developments permitted development, but this has yet to happen.

Outbuildings and enclosures

This includes garages, car ports, sheds, workshops, greenhouses, tennis court fences, summerhouses and swimming pool enclosures. An unlimited number of such buildings can be built on your land without the need to obtain planning permission provided that you comply with the following:

■ Position: No outbuilding should be built closer to any highway than any part of the existing house, unless the distance between the outbuilding and the highway is 20m or more.

■ No more than half of the area of land around the original house should be covered by such outbuildings (or extensions).

■ Outbuildings positioned within five metres of the house will be considered as extensions for the purposes of permitted development.

■ Size: Within those areas described in designated areas (above), any outbuilding of more than ten cubic metres in size, anywhere in the garden of the house, will require planning permission and will also count as an extension and be deducted from the permitted development allowance for extensions. Outside those areas there are no restrictions on the actual size of the outbuildings constructed, other than in terms of height and position.

■ Height: Buildings or structures should not be more than three metres in height or four metres if the building has a ridged (ie pitched) roof.

■ Think ahead: Be careful not to construct outbuildings where they would prevent future permitted development extensions.

Remember that if an extension comes closer than 5m to an existing outbuilding, that outbuilding would count, itself, as an extension in terms of the permitted development allowance.

Use of outbuildings for residential purposes

Existing outbuildings can be used to provide ancillary living accommodation (for sleeping, eating, washing etc) provided that no actual change of use takes place:

■ The outbuilding is not used as a separate dwelling.

■ The outbuilding is used only as an annexe to the main house by a member of the household.

■ The use of the outbuilding is tied up with, and closely related to, the use of the main house as a single private dwelling.

This means that, while the accommodation of an elderly dependent relative in a detached annexe may be acceptable, the use of the outbuilding to provide a cheap home for grown up children would not. If you encounter difficulty in taking this approach, it may be useful to draw the planner's attention to the case of Uttlesford District Council v Secretary of State for the Environment and White, March 1991, which is found in the Journal of Planning Law 1992. Although an existing out building can be used for ancillary accommodation, provided it does not constitute a change of use, it is not lawful to build an outbuilding for the express purpose of providing self contained accommodation as that would not be permitted development.

Domestic heating oil storage tanks

These should not exceed 3500 litres in capacity, be more than three metres above ground level and not come between the house and the road. Liquefied petroleum gas tanks will always require planning permission.

Porches

You may put a porch on any of the doors to your house provided that:

■ Position: It is at least two metres away from the highway.

■ Size: It does not exceed three cubic metres in ground floor area, measured externally.

■ Height: It does not exceed three metres in height.

Fences, walls and gates

The right to build, repair or reposition a fence or wall does not relate to the type of materials used. Planning permission is not required provided that:

■ Height: No fence or wall should exceed one metre in height where it is situated directly adjacent to a highway. Elsewhere the maximum height for fences on the boundary of properties is two metres.

■ Position: The phrase adjacent to the highway means near to the edge of the highway. Different planning authorities operate different interpretations of what this means. In my view if a fence is further than two metres from the highway it is not adjacent to it.

■ Safety: If you are erecting or repositioning a fence, be careful to avoid blocking sight lines causing lack of visibility at road junctions. In such cases the local authority can decide that permission is required due to the effect on highway safety. On many estates, fences are deliberately set back to provide adequate visibility for cars and this may be controlled by a condition on the planning permission for the development.

■ Trees and hedges

Planning permission is not usually required to enclose a garden with trees or hedges, provided that a condition does not exist which specifically prevents it. Such a condition may exist to prevent the blocking of sight lines at road junctions or in other locations where visibility is important.

Access

You do not need planning permission to create an access from the road onto your property providing that the road is not a trunk or classified road and that the access does not obstruct sight lines or cause danger.

In creating the new access, permission to cross the pavement or verge will be required from the Highways Authority (usually the county council or, in London, the relevant borough) who will also stipulate the method of construction of the dropped kerb, or pavement crossover.

Driveways, hard standings and patios

There are no restrictions on the right to create hard surfaces on all or part of your garden, although such hard surfaces must only be used in connection with the private use of the house.

Parking

■ Caravans: Planning permission is not required to park a caravan in the front or back garden of a house provided that it is not used as separate living accommodation, independent of the house itself.

■ Commercial vehicles: If the homeowner uses a commercial vehicle as part of their job and parks it at home, overnight and at weekends (as one would a private car) then planning permission may not be required. However, the use of a private house as the base for operating a commercial vehicle business (like a taxi or van hire business) does require permission.

Integral garages

Permission is not required to convert an integral or attached garage into a room used as part of the house (unless this is prevented by a condition).

Swimming pools and ponds

Planning permission is not required to create swimming pools or ponds within the garden provided that they, in combination with all extensions and outbuildings, would not cover more than half the area of land around the original house. Any building over a pool would be considered in the same way as any other outbuilding.

Satellite dishes

Provided that certain rules are complied with, permission is not required for a satellite dish, although it is important that the dish is sited to minimise its visual impact. This is clearly a matter of opinion, so before installing a dish, gain the planning authority's agreement in writing that the site you have chosen is the one which does minimize the visual impact of the dish.

In all areas:

■ Only one dish is permitted.

■ It must not protrude above the highest part of the roof.

■ If located on a chimney, it must not exceed 45cm in diameter or be above the highest part of the chimney stack.

In the following counties, the maximum size of dish permitted is 90cm:

Cleveland, Cornwall, Cumbria, Devon, Durham, Dyfed, Greater Manchester, Gwynedd, Humberside, Lancashire, Merseyside, Northumberland, North Yorkshire, South Yorkshire, Tyne and Wear, West Glamorgan, West Yorkshire.

Outside these counties, the maximum size permitted is 70cm. If a house is located in a national park, area of outstanding natural beauty, conservation area or the Norfolk Broads, then in addition to these rules:

■ The dish must not be located on a chimney.

■ The dish must not be positioned on a wall or roof slope fronting a road or public footpath (or waterway in the Broads).

Satellite dishes on flats

For larger blocks of flats (more than 15 metres in height or approximately five stories) outside national parks, areas of outstanding natural beauty, conservation areas or the Norfolk Broads, two dishes in total are permitted for the whole block. Each must not exceed 90cm. If the block is located within the above areas, then planning permission is required.

For smaller blocks of flats, one dish is permitted for the whole block. Clearly, once one or two people have erected a dish on a block of flats, then further dishes will require planning permission. This generally means that erecting dishes on flats will often only be possible on a 'first come first served' basis.

Running a business or working from home

The planning situation regarding the use of a house for business purposes is not governed by simple legislation. A considerable amount of judgement is involved. The basic principle is that planning permission is not usually needed if the character and use of the building remains essentially residential. Planning permission will be needed if the character and use of the house changes so that it is no longer essentially, and predominantly, residential. Therefore, it is usually possible, without planning permission to:

■ Use part of a house to rent to a lodger or for bed and breakfast accommodation.

■ Use a room as a personal office (for those who work from home).

■ Provide a small-scale child minding service or playgroup.

■ Use a room for a business such as music teaching, hairdressing or an employment agency, for example.

■ Use a garage to repair cars occasionally or store goods connected with a business.

Clearly all the above activities could be carried out at widely different levels of intensity or scale. The use of a house without planning permission implies that the activities should be small scale and not cause disturbance. The following considerations will be important:

■ The house should be used predominantly and substantially as a private domestic residence.

■ There should not be a significant increase in traffic or visitors to the house. For instance, an employment agency based on the phone may be acceptable, while one involving regular visitors would require permission.

■ The business should not involve any activities out of place in a residential area, so disturbing neighbours by creating noise or smells.

■ If anyone, other than the residents of the house, is being employed in the business then planning permission may be needed.

The basic test as to whether working from home will require permission is whether the changes in activity involved would be disruptive in a residential area. If not, and the house remains predominantly residential, then permission will not usually be needed.

A business started at home without requiring planning permission may go on to expand. If the level of activity rises then it could be argued that planning permission is required. A pragmatic way of dealing with this could be to let the local planning department make the decision for you. Once it starts receiving complaints, it will contact you to request an application or instruct you to stop. Government advice is that businesses should not be excluded from residential areas without good reason, so you may be wise in pursuing your case to appeal. It would not be an offence to carry on the business until the result of the appeal is issued unless the local authority has served a stop notice on you.

Shared houses

Planning permission will not normally be required to use a house to provide rented accommodation, for instance, to students. However, the number of people living together must not exceed six. They must also, to quote the legislation, be living together 'as a family', sharing facilities such as kitchens, bathrooms and sitting rooms. If the number exceeds six, or self-contained bedsits are created, then planning permission may be required for a change of use. The environmental health department of the local authority can also provide you with help as to what constitutes a house in multi-occupation and what non-planning controls apply.

Maintenance and repairs

Planning permission does not need to be obtained for the following:

■ Internal alterations.

■ Repairs and maintenance: This includes re-roofing a house, provided that there is no change in the shape or height.

■ Painting or decorating the outside of the house: If a house is located in any of the areas listed in designated areas above, then planning permission is required to clad the outside with stone, tile, artificial stone, plastic or timber. Elsewhere permission is not required to do this.

Demolition and rebuilding

■ Demolition: Outside conservation areas, planning permission is not required to demolish any building of less than 50 cubic metres (measured externally). The demolition of any building used as a dwelling, or attached to a dwelling which exceeds this size, may require a planning application. I would recommend that if you wish to demolish all or part of a house, that you provide details of what you intend to do and seek the advice of your local planning department.

■ Demolition in conservation areas: Conservation area consent is required for the total or substantial demolition of any unlisted building with a total cubic content exceeding 115 cubic metres, using external measurements, in a conservation area. The definition of substantial is not necessarily clear so I would strongly recommend that, if you intend to demolish any building in a conservation area that you liaise closely with the conservation officer, and/or a planning consultant. This is because unauthorised demolition is a criminal offence and what is unauthorised may be a matter of the conservation officer's opinion.

■ Rebuilding: If a building is demolished and you intend to rebuild it in exactly the same form, subject to the note on Original House above, planning permission is still required. What is more, it will not necessarily be granted. The proposed new building will be judged as if it were any other new proposal. If the original building caused the problems of overlooking or overshadowing or looked ugly, the planners are likely to want to improve matters.

Scotland

Permitted development rights in Scotland are similar to those in England, in general terms, but they are expressed in square rather than cubic metres. The following are some examples of the more commonly encountered types of domestic permitted development. They are subject to the amount that a house has already been enlarged, as in England, and may have been used up.

Examples of permitted development

■ Detached and semi-detached houses: Planning permission is not required for extensions which do not exceed 24 sq metres or 20 per cent of the floor area of the original house, whichever is the greater, up to a maximum of 30 sq metres. Extensions must not exceed the height of the highest part of the existing roof. Extensions must not extend beyond the building line facing a road if within 20 metres of that road.

■ Terraced houses and houses in conservation areas: Planning permission is not required for extensions which do not exceed 16 sq metres in area or 10 per cent of the area of the original house, whichever is the greater, up to maximum of 30 sq metres. As in England, extensions must not exceed the height of the highest part of the existing roof or extend beyond the building line facing a road if within 20 metres of the edge of the highway, which may be closer than the actual road surface itself.

■ Flats: As in England, flats do not have 'permitted development' rights other than in relation to a limited ability to install satellite dishes and planning permission is therefore needed for any extension.

■ Outbuildings: Outbuildings of four square metres, and within five metres of any part of the dwelling, shall be treated as the enlargement of the dwelling for all purposes and so use up the available permitted development allowance. Equally, though, they can be considered to form part of the original house when working out what permitted development is available.

Outbuildings more than five metres away from any dwelling are limited to four metres in the case of a building with a ridged roof; or three metres in any other case. The total area of ground covered by buildings or enclosures within the curtilage (other than the original dwelling) should not exceed 30 per cent of the total area of the curtilage (excluding the ground area of the original dwelling). In the case of any land in a conservation area, or land within the curtilage of a listed building, it would consist of the provision, alteration or improvement of a building with a floor area greater than four square metres.

■ Porches: Unlike in England, where porches are a separate class of permitted development, in Scotland they are treated as an extension and so any porch protruding beyond the building line (within 20 metress of a public highway) will require planning permission.

■ Dormer Windows: Unlike England, all dormer windows always require planning permission. Roof-lights are permitted development provided they do not stand more than 10 cms above the roof slope.

■ Future Changes in Scotland: The permitted development rights in Scotland are currently being reviewed. For more information on this and for chapter and verse on the actual regulations, visit www.scotland. gov.uk/Publications/2006/10/09103423/0. This is a link to the report presenting the findings from the Stage 1 review of the General Permitted Development Order as it affects householder developments.

Written confirmation or lawful development certificate

If, having considered this section, you think that what you want to do is permitted development, then you may write to your local planning authority and request written confirmation that planning permission is not required. Such informal confirmation is not binding on an authority and, as such, its use is limited. However, it can provide some peace of mind and will enable you to demonstrate to neighbours that everything is in order and to provide evidence when selling your house that the extensions or alterations made were legitimate.

Some authorities no longer provide such letters and would insist that you apply for a lawful development certificate. Where there is no confusion and where permitted development is very clear, a lawful development certificate is overkill. A letter from a professional chartered planning consultant, confirming to you that something is permitted development, could be used to keep lenders or future buyers happy. It can also be a useful half way house between a lawful development certificate or nothing if the council will not provide a letter of comfort

.

If the council will respond informally then in your letter, provide the following information (if you have it and it is relevant in your case):

■ Your address.

■ Whether your house has been extended (since July 1948).

■ Whether your house is terraced.

■ The size and position of the building you wish to construct.

■ Whether the proposed building will be within two metres of your garden boundary.

■ Whether the proposed extension will be within five metres of any existing outbuilding (or vice versa).

It is often helpful to provide some of the information in the form of a sketch, indicating the relevant distances between house, outbuildings, road and boundary in metres.

If the proposal is not considered to be permitted development, find out from the planning office exactly why not. It may be that minor adjustments to the size or position of the proposal would be sufficient to render it as permitted development.

Appendix II
LISTED BUILDINGS AND CONSERVATION AREAS

The protection of historic buildings is not covered by planning legislation but by the closely related parallel system of listed building control. So, if you are involved in a development including a listed building it is likely that you will need both planning permission and listed building consent. The determination of both applications will be made on the basis of different, but related, criteria. Development plans rarely have policies concerning listed buildings; if they do have policies they tend to just be the repetition of government advice. The criteria used to judge listed buildings focuses on their architectural and historic value. It does not include planning concerns such as residential amenity, highway safety, or housing policy. These may all be relevant as part of the associated planning application but do not have a bearing on the acceptability, or otherwise, of the specific works to a listed building.

The issues related to listed buildings are set out fully in PPG15 and are summarised as follows:

i. the importance of the building, its intrinsic architectural and historic interest and rarity, in both national and local terms ('historic interest' is further explained in paragraph 6.11);

ii. the particular physical features of the building (which may include its design, plan, materials or location) which justify its inclusion in the list: list descriptions may draw attention to features of particular interest or value, but they are not exhaustive and other features of importance (eg interiors) may come to light after the building's inclusion in the list;

iii. the building's setting and its contribution to the local scene, which may be very important, eg. where it forms an element in a group, park, garden or other townscape or landscape, or where it shares particular architectural forms or details with other buildings nearby;

iv. the extent to which the proposed works would bring substantial benefits for the community, in particular by contributing to the economic regeneration of the area or the enhancement of its environment (including other listed buildings).

Listed building legislation is far more restrictive than laws relating to planning. To carry out unauthorised works on a listed building is a criminal offence and there is no four or ten year rule that will provide eventual immunity from enforcement. In Scotland, it is Historic Scotland who administers the listed building legislation at the national level. In Wales, the National Assembly for Wales is ultimately responsible for historic buildings and published policy guidance sets out the planning framework (Welsh Office Circulars 61/96 and 1/98).

Why are buildings listed?

The buildings are considered to be 'special' on the basis of either 'architectural' or 'historic' interest, or both, and are assessed for listing against the criteria published in Planning Policy Guidance Note 15 on Planning and the Historic Environment. These are:

■ Architectural interest: The lists are meant to include all buildings, which are of importance to the nation for the interest of their architectural design, decoration and craftsmanship; also important examples of particular building types and techniques (e.g. buildings displaying technical innovation or virtuosity) and significant plan forms.

■ Historic interest: This includes buildings which display important

aspects of the nation's social, economic, cultural or military history.

■ Close historical associations with nationally important people or events.

■ Group value: Especially where buildings comprise together an important architectural or historical unity or a fine example of planning (e.g. squares, terraces or model villages).

As a general rule:
■ All buildings built before 1700 that survive in anything like their original condition will be listed.

■ Most buildings from 1700 to 1840 are listed but there is some selection. For example if a building of this period is very much altered it will not be included.

■ Buildings from 1840 to 1914 need to have some particular quality and character. In this group the works of principal architects come into play.

■ Buildings from 1914 to date must be of a very high quality to be included.

It's not just buildings that are listed. Structures such as garden walls, railings, gates, statues, grottoes, milestones, tombs, gravestones and bridges can all be listed individually.

NB Listing relates both to the exterior and interior of a building, to any object or structure fixed to it and any structure within its curtilage, which forms part of the land and has done so since before 1 July 1948.

Grades of listed building

In England and Wales
Virtually all pre-1700 buildings that survive in anything like their original condition are listed, as are most buildings between 1700 and 1840. The

criteria are more selective for buildings after 1840, depending upon their contribution, features or history. Local authorities and the relevant county council hold a register of listed buildings with an entry for each property, but this is only a guide to some of the main features. The categories of listing are as follows:

Grade I   Buildings of exceptional interest and outstanding national significance. There are roughly 6,000 of these in the UK.

Grade II*   Particularly important buildings which are of more than special interest.

Grade II   Buildings of special interest that justify every effort being made to preserve them.

There are some 500,000 Grade II* and Grade II buildings in the UK.
The owner of a Grade I building will be subject to the strongest controls on what work is acceptable or not, but is rewarded with the greater likelihood of financial support. English Heritage tend to be directly involved with Grade I and II* buildings.

In Scotland

Historic Scotland assigns each listed building to one of three categories to reflect their degree of interest.

Category A: Buildings of national or international importance, either architectural or historic, or fine little-altered examples of some particular period, style or building type.

Category B: Buildings of regional or more than local importance, or major examples of some particular period, style or building type, which may have been altered.

Category C(S): Buildings of local importance, lesser examples of any period, style or building type, as originally constructed or altered; and simple, traditional buildings, which group well with others in categories A and B or are part

of a planned group such as an estate or an industrial complex.

At present, Scotland has about 47,000 listed buildings. These cover a very wide range of building types and styles.

The listing process

Applications for adding a building to the statutory list in England must be sent direct to English Heritage, who will notify owners and local authorities. It is their intention to introduce clearer information for owners of listed buildings. English Heritage is responsible for inspecting properties and providing advice for the Secretary of State.

■ Applicants who want a building added to, or removed from, the list apply directly to English Heritage. English Heritage will make an assessment of the building against set criteria and a recommendation to list, de-list or amend the grade will be made to the Secretary of State at the Department of Culture Media and Sport.

■ English Heritage is required to notify owners if an application to list their building is made by another party. Previously owners were not necessarily informed.

■ English Heritage will then consult the owners and relevant local authorities on applications to list buildings.

English Heritage intends to introduce clearer information for owners and managers of listed buildings so that they will benefit from precise information about what the listing of their property means. It is intended that information packs for owners, which give more detailed guidance about the implications of listing and sources of expert advice, will be sent to all owners of newly listed buildings in the near future.

For further details, please visit the English Heritage website: www. english-heritage.org.uk

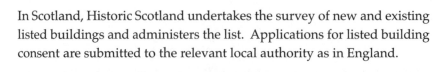

In Scotland, Historic Scotland undertakes the survey of new and existing listed buildings and administers the list. Applications for listed building consent are submitted to the relevant local authority as in England.

In Wales the Secretary of State for Wales acts on recommendations from CADW (Welsh(Welsh Historic Monuments).

In England, English Heritage (in Scotland, Historic Scotland, in Wales, CADW) is responsible for considering and advising on all applications for listing and for making recommendations to the Secretary of State about whether to add buildings to the statutory list.

English Heritage will assess the building against the criteria published in Planning Policy Guidance 15: Planning and the Historic Environment. This planning policy guidance is well worth looking at by anyone who owns a historic building. If there is any doubt about the significance of the building, English Heritage may undertake historical and documentary research and make comparisons with other examples of the same building type. In most cases an inspection will be undertaken, although this is not always necessary. Where English Heritage considers that an inspection is desirable, the owner's permission will be sought.

When the assessment is complete, and any comments from the owner and local authority considered, the recommendation will be forwarded to the Department for Culture, Media and Sport (in England). Before taking a decision, the Secretary of State may seek advice from acknowledged experts in the field. After the Secretary of State has come to a decision, the owner, applicant and local authority will be notified, and sent a letter detailing the reasons for the decision.

Permitted development

A listed house that has not been extended or enlarged since 1947 will still have its full complement of permitted development rights. So planning permission will not be required to do the normal small-scale extensions. However, listed building consent will be required, so you may end up making just a listed building consent application to carry out works that would otherwise be entirely permitted development.

Total protection

It is important to remember that listed buildings are not just protected on the outside. The inside, including all internal fittings, joinery and fabric is also covered. It is a common misapprehension among people in the development industry that a building can be listed in part or that only particular features mentioned in the listed description are protected. This is entirely wrong. The listed description found on the statutory list is simply there to identify the building. The omission or inclusion of any internal or external feature in the description does not necessarily have any bearing on its degree of importance as part of the building.

Building preservation notices

Planning authorities and National Park authorities have the power to serve a building preservation notice on the owner of a building which is not listed, but which they consider is of special architectural or historic interest and is in danger of demolition or potentially harmful alterations.

A building preservation notice provides six month's protection to a building as if it were listed. This allows time for a full assessment to be carried out. The planning authority usually serves a building preservation notice on the owner of the building and then notifies the Secretary of State, requesting that the building be considered for listing. The Secretary of State then has six months to decide whether to list the building. If it is not listed, compensation may be payable if any financial loss has been sustained as a result of the building preservation notice. So, as you can imagine, they are not served lightly.

Certificates of Immunity

A certificate of immunity precludes the Secretary of State from listing a

building and prevents the planning authority from serving a building preservation notice for five years. Provided that planning permission is being sought, or has been obtained, any person may ask the Secretary of State to issue a certificate of immunity. The certificate is a useful tool where development is intended on a site. It gives greater certainty to developers proposing works which will affect buildings that may be eligible for listing. If a certificate of immunity is not issued, then a building will normally be added to the statutory list.

Applying for listed building consent

Listed building consent is required in order to carry out any works to a listed building, which will affect its special value for listing purposes. This will almost certainly be necessary for any major works, but may also be necessary for minor alterations and possibly even repairs and maintenance. Listed building consent may also be necessary for a change of use of the property. What actually requires consent will often, in reality, be at the discretion of the council's conservation officer, not in law but in day-to-day practice, as it is they who will advise you about changes and repairs that you may carry out. What will or will not affect the historic integrity or interest of the building will always, to some extent, be a matter of judgment and different conservation officers can take a different line.

Works such as re-pointing and even repainting can give rise to the need for a listed building consent, even if planning permission is not necessary. Replacement windows and doors are common areas of controversy and strict control.

Identical repairs carried out in the correct traditional manner in matching materials may not require consent, but it is always strongly advisable to check with the council's listed buildings, or conservation officer, (usually in the planning department) before undertaking any work.

Applications for listed building consent are made in a similar fashion to normal planning applications on a form that can be obtained from your local planning department. If you need planning permission for your intended proposal, then the two applications can be submitted together. There is no fee for the listed building consent application. Listed building applications now require design and access statements, as per normal planning applications, to justify what is proposed.

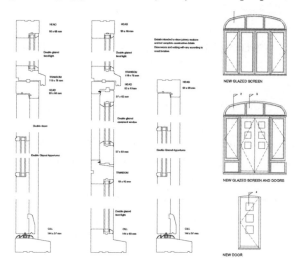

High levels of detail will be required to demonstrate the nature of all the proposed alterations, including internal joinery and detailing. It is these small scale elements that create the character of an early building and can be so easily lost.

The application form will set out the information required, which will normally include:

■ A site plan to 1/1250 or 1/2500 scale showing the property.

■ A description of the works being applied for.

■ A set of existing and proposed scale drawings, including elevations, internal floor plans and much more detail than is required for a planning application. For major works, or those involving a particularly early or important building, you will need to involve an architect or designer with experience of works to listed buildings.

■ The application will be processed in the same way as planning application and the council will approve, approve with conditions or refuse the application.

■ There are similar rights to appeal against a refusal or conditions as for other planning applications.

An LBC application of any size may also need to contain an above-ground archaeological appraisal of the building and full schedule of works. More details can be obtained by reference to planning policy guidance Note 15 (PPG15) Planning and the Historic Environment.

Financial help for maintenance of a listed building

Some owners of listed buildings think that they are automatically entitled to a grant towards maintaining their historic pile. Although local authorities do have the power to give grants, they rarely do. Grants for the repair of buildings of outstanding architectural or historic interest, (which usually means grades I and II*) may be available through English Heritage providing that the application is made prior to the work being carried out. All applications for grant assistance are judged on their individual merits. English Heritage takes into account the importance of the building, the urgency of the proposed repairs and the need for financial support. In some areas they are, in effect, means tested.

There are a number of charitable trusts that you may wish to consult about award grants towards the preservation and upkeep of historic buildings. Further details of these can be found in the Directory of Grant Making Trusts published by the Charities Aid Foundation, which is available from 114-118 Southampton Row, London, WC1B 5AA.

Removing a building from the statutory list

The Secretary of State will remove a building from the list if it no longer meets the statutory criteria. This may be because of new evidence about the special architectural or historic interest of the building, or a material change of circumstances (for example, fire damage that has affected the special interest of the building). The Secretary of State can only take into account a building's architectural or historic interest when considering an application for de-listing.

Applications for de-listing will not usually be considered if the building is currently the subject of an application for listed building consent, or an appeal against refusal of consent, or if action by a local planning authority is underway. This is because both listed building consent and enforcement appeal procedures give appellants the right to argue that a building is not of special interest and should be removed from the list. Where this process is already underway, the issue of de-listing can be addressed that way. Ironically, once listed barns have received consent for conversion to houses, the results can sometimes lead to successful de-listing.

Applications for de-listing should be made to English Heritage in the same way as listing applications.

Conservation areas

Conservation areas are largely misunderstood by the general public who seem to believe that this designation will prevent change. The reality is that conservation areas are designated as they represent parts of towns or villages that represent 'areas of special architectural or historic interest the character and appearance of which it is desirable to preserve or enhance' (Planning Policy Guidance Note 15).

Sometimes rather ropy areas can be designated as the local authority hope that conservation area status will lead to improvements. The two main additional powers available to a planning authority in a conservation area are firstly the requirement for conservation area consent for the total demolition of any building whose cubic content is greater than 115 square metres. The second power is the reduction in the amount of permitted development that can be built.

Local authorities have a duty to draw up conservation area appraisals that they subject to a degree of local consultation then adopt as supplementary planning guidance to help identify what key features of an area will be worth preserving and what the predominant local architectural and urban design characteristics are. Not all local authorities have got around to doing these statements but they can be very helpful if you are contemplating making an application for development. It is particularly useful to see if they have identified your site as an important open space that should be preserved, or not.

So any application that is submitted for a new development in a conservation area will be looked at very carefully by the local authority. It will want to be convinced that the proposal will either preserve or enhance the character and appearance of that area. A lot of emphasis will be placed on the existing nature of the location, the way the proposal responds to that and how well the architecture is justified in its context. This means that a good designer and careful presentation of the scheme will be the key to success.

I often feel that conservation area status can create more, rather than less, of an opportunity for new development. This is because so much of the debate will revolve around what should be built in architectural terms so there is scope for innovative and imaginative designs that may be harder to justify in a less sensitive urban or rural location. Conservation areas do require special treatment but they need not be a barrier to development.

The very new next to the very old, sometimes a favourite of conservation officers, the plans and the finished job enable you to judge if it works.

Appendix III
TREES & TREE PRESERVATION ORDERS

Trees may be protected in three ways:
- By a tree preservation order (TPO)
- By being located in a conservation area
- By a planning condition.

Tree preservation orders

Councils may protect trees they consider of value by serving a tree preservation order (TPO). This can be served on anything from individual trees in private gardens to extensive woodlands. Works to trees under the protection of a TPO can only be carried out with the Councils consent. The exceptions to this are when:

- The tree is dead, dying or dangerous

- The tree has to be cut down or pruned in connection with the work of a statutory body, such as the electricity board or water authority

- The tree has to be removed as part of a development that has been granted planning permission by the council. This is assuming that the tree's removal is specifically mentioned as part of that approved scheme

A TPO allows the council's officers to make sure that proposals to prune

a tree are necessary and will not harm its health or appearance. Any tree that becomes threatened and is deemed worthy by the council can be covered by a TPO. The initial order is provisional for six months while the council considers any objections to it. If there are none within twenty eight days the order can be confirmed straight away. If there are objections the order should be confirmed, or not, within six months following discussion with the complainant.

If a tree subject to an order is removed, deliberately killed or damaged, the planning authority can prosecute the person carrying out the work and the resulting fine can be set in relation to the commercial gain achieved by carrying out the unauthorised felling or works. In certain circumstances the removal of a preserved tree may be agreed, but the owner will usually be required to replace the tree with one of an agreed species and size. Fruit trees cultivated on a commercial basis are not subject to TPOs

A TPO has to be served on everyone who has a legal interest in the land involved. Any of these people have a right of appeal to the council against the inclusion of trees in an order – but in practice you will need to be supported by evidence from a qualified arboricultural consultant.

Details of TPOs within your area can be obtained from the planning department. Applications for the felling or pruning of protected trees should be in the form of a letter stating the location and species of tree, and the type of work proposed. No fee is required.

Trees in conservation areas

All trees in conservation areas are subject to extra protection. Those not already included in a TPO may only be pruned or felled after the council has been given six weeks written notice. This period allows the council to assess the tree's visual importance and to make a TPO if necessary.

Planning conditions

When these exist on the site of a proposal, then conditions will often be

attached to ensure that the trees are protected during construction works and are not removed. Quite often conditions will be used to ensure the planting of additional trees on a site. Planning conditions are useful in planting, maintaining and protecting trees in the short term but they do not offer real long-term protection in the same way as a TPO.

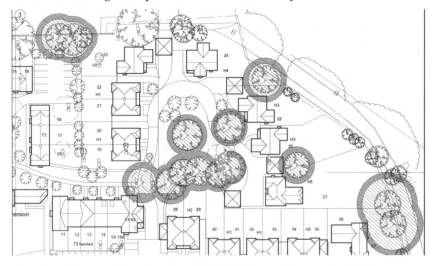

Thias housing layout has been specifically designed to accomodate the protected trees on the site ringed in dark grey in this drawing).

Trees and your planning application

The presence of large trees in your garden can have a significant impact on your ability to extend your house. If trees are attractive and visually important in an area, then it is quite possible that permission for extensions will be refused in order to prevent their loss.

Points to remember:

■ Always check before felling or making substantial surgery on a mature tree that it is not the subject of a TPO. If it is, then you could face substantial fines unless you first obtain the consent of your local authority

■ A TPO is overridden by a planning application where the removal of the tree is specified

■ Many trees, although not under a TPO, may be protected by conditions attached to previous planning permissions

Find out if you are in a conservation area.

Trees and building works

■ Trees should be carefully protected during building works in accordance with BS 5837 (2005), avoid the storage of building materials or top soil under trees

■ No machinery, particularly cement mixers, should be placed under trees. No vehicles should be parked or driven under trees as this causes damaging soil compaction

■ Rising or lowering soil levels under the branch spread of trees can cause serious damage to their health

■ Wherever possible all building works and ground disturbance should be done outside the branch spread of trees

■ Avoid cutting any tree roots larger than two inches in diameter

Can you appeal against a Tree Preservation Order?

The legislation provides no right of appeal to the Secretary of State against the actual serving of a TPO. The validity of a TPO can only be challenged by way of application to the High Court. This must be done only in relation to a point of law with in 6 weeks of the confirmation of the order.

However all is not lost if you do think an existing TPO is unjustified or pointless (for example due to the life or health of a tree) as an appeal to the Secretary of State can be made following an application to cut down or carry out work on trees protected by a TPO. This must be made within 28 days of receiving the councils refusal to allow such works.

Appendix IV
HOW TO OBJECT TO AN APPLICATION

There are three reasons why it is useful to object to an application with which you disagree.

■ You may draw attention to problems caused by the proposal which the planning officers may otherwise overlook.

■ In a borderline case, when the proposal is considered just acceptable, your objection could swing the balance in favour of refusal.

■ You may influence the elected councillors, who may consequently refuse the application.

Finding out about the application

In some districts, you will be personally notified by card or letter about an application made by one of your neighbours. In other districts, the application may be advertised by means of a notice (usually orange) pinned up on the site for a minimum of 21 days. In all areas a list of planning applications will be placed regularly in one or more local papers. If you are unclear what is intended, get advice from a planning officer. Make sure you find out the last date for objections to be received. This will usually be the day before the relevant planning committee. Planning authorities are legally obliged to inform any objectors to a proposal about

the outcome of the planning application.

How do you object?

Applicants generally seem to be far more offended by objectors who complain immediately to the council than by those who approach them in person. It is therefore sensible, in the first instance, to talk directly to the applicant and diplomatically explain your concerns. This might not change anything but it could avoid a neighbourhood feud. When objecting to the council always do so in writing and quote the application number. Talk to your local councillor and explain your concerns; provide them with a copy of your letter. In some parts of the country, objectors are allowed to speak directly to the planning committee. In other areas, objectors may address a small pre-meeting to express their concerns. In most cases, objections can only be made in writing and verbally to planning officers or councillors during the weeks prior to the committee.

Groups of protestors sometimes get together and organise a petition against a particular proposal. In my view such lists of signatures are fairly easy to collect in large numbers and are not nearly as effective as individual letters of objection.

What do you say?

It is best to confirm your comments to those that are relevant to planning – these things are called material considerations. If you do include objections that are not relevant in planning terms they will be ignored, but they may have the unwanted effect of directing attention away from your valid objections.

The following are not generally considered 'material' to the determination of an application, so you would (usually) be wasting effort complaining about them:

■ A fall in the value of your property.

■ The loss of an attractive general view from your particular house.

■ Your speculations ('this may be the thin end of the wedge').

■ A lot of recent development in your area.

■ Commercial harm from additional competition to your business.

■ That the development was initially done without permission.

■ Personal dislike or suspicion of the applicant or his intentions.

In contrast, the most relevant considerations in planning terms (therefore the ones which you should use) include:

■ The physical impact of the proposal in terms of:
Loss of privacy.
Loss of sunlight.
The effect on the immediate view from your windows.
Creating a dominating and oppressive effect over your house or garden.

■ The physical effects in more general terms such as:
Design out of character with the surrounding area.
Creation of a damaging precedent, which would encourage similar applications elsewhere, which would individually and collectively harm the area.

■ Similarity with previous applications, which were refused (either on the same property or elsewhere).

■ Loss of or damage to attractive trees.

■ Poor materials.

■ Excessive height in comparison with other buildings in the area.

■ Loss of important views into open countryside (when part of the village or town's character).

■ Loss of attractive green spaces within built up area.

■ Creation of an excessively high-density development out of character with the surrounding area.

How do you say it?

When writing a letter of objection, begin by quoting the planning application number, the relevant address and description of the proposal.

■ Consider carefully what you intend to say.

■ Don't ramble and include irrelevant information.

■ Don't be emotional and make personal comments about the applicant.

■ Don't exaggerate, be honest and realistic.

■ Set out the reasons for your objections one by one and follow each with brief details.

■ Type the letter.

Appendix V
FREQUENTLY ASKED QUESTIONS

How long will a planning application take?

The simple, theoretical answer is eight weeks. This is known as the 'statutory period' for the determination of a planning application. It is eight weeks for minor applications and 13 weeks for major proposals, if an application is not determined within these time periods then an applicant is entitled to appeal against non-determination, although as an appeal will take at least 6 months there is usually not much point. The definition of major includes applications of 10 or more houses.

Local authorities are subject to very careful scrutiny by the government and have to provide regular reports as to performance in meeting these targets. Failure to meet them can result in a reduction in funding and ultimately direct intervention by the government in the running of the planning department. The intention of course is to ensure that local authorities deal with applications quickly and on the face of it this might appear to be a good idea. The government likes it as there are now statistics, set out in a league table for England and Wales, that indicate how efficient local authorities are.

The reality is entirely different and the obsession with targets has resulted in a system in which it takes much longer to get permission. The system has become process-driven not outcome-driven. The very quick determination of an application is always easy when it is a refusal,

arriving at a negotiated solution takes longer. The eight week period only measures a small section of the process of achieving a positive outcome and very few planning authorities are prepared to sacrifice targets in order to negotiate during the life of an application.

The planning process starts with the instruction of an architectural designer to draw up a scheme that will eventually be submitted in the form of an application. The government encourage pre-application discussions and negotiations with the planning authority and other interested bodies such as the high authority, environmental health officers, environment agency and anyone else who may be consulted on the subsequent planning application.

All this takes an indeterminate length of time and the more complex a site the longer it takes but because such informal discussions are not monitored in the same way as the statutory period they are not accorded the same level of priority. If there's a problem once an application is submitted the proposal is usually either very quickly refused or the planning authority may indicate that there is an issue that needs resolution and will provide the opportunity for the applicant to withdraw and start again with a new statutory period.

So if you're considering the time period needed for an option agreement or conditional contract to buy land I would suggest a minimum six month period for a planning application followed by one year to deal with any subsequent planning appeal.

How much will obtaining planning permission cost?

The application fee submitted to a local authority is probably the least expensive part of making a planning application. A detailed application for residential development requires a fee of just under £300 per house. An outline application is based on the site area and is a similar amount per 0.1 of a hectare with no maximum fee. The real price of the application is the cost of the professional advice and services required to produce the necessary plans and supporting statements.

In recent years planning has become more bureaucratic and complex and most applications, other than small domestic proposals, now require a design and access statement. This sets out a justification of the design approach taken and presents an argument as to why a site is reasonably located in accessibility terms.

Where there are highways issues of road safety and access geometry, technical advice may be needed. If there are drainage issues or potential contaminated land concerns money will be spent on professional expertise.

It is no longer possible to make a bare outline planning application which contains little or no detail as the current version of the 'outline' application requires almost the same level of information as a full and detailed proposal. The cost of the designer or architect will be critical and it is advisable to ensure that the agreed fees include at least some acknowledgement of the need to revise proposals and amended plans.

One of the hidden costs of making a planning application results from the delays often inherent in the system; if land has been bought with borrowed money, or the purchase price is index linked, then the longer the process takes the more it costs. When thinking about your budget to cover professional fees think carefully about this and the range of expertise needed to deal with all the technical matters involved in the submission, starting with an accurate topographical and tree survey of the site.

The costs of getting permission do not end once the decision notice has been received. As part of the application process it is highly likely that you will be requested to enter into a Section 106 Agreement to provide financial contributions towards a wide range of local services.

In theory this is money to pay for the added burden on the provision of services through the additional population growth resulting from the houses that are being built. The list of recipients of this money is ever-growing, it normally includes the education department of the local authority, the highways department, the library service, the recreational

providers, even the local fire brigade and of course the provision of affordable housing either on site or by financial contribution.

There is a strong suspicion amongst many developers that it is simply a local tax, soon to be increased and added to by a national development tax. For developers, the amounts required currently range from between £1000 to £20,000 per house. It seems to me that they normally pitch it at a level which is just about less painful than waiting a year trying to reduce it via a planning appeal. Government advice emphasises that the amounts to paid will be negotiated – which is a neat way of pointing out that local authorities will normally ask for more than expect to get. The payments set out in the Section 106 Agreement are normally payable upon the commencement of development and in real terms do comprise part of the cost of getting the permission.

Will the council tell me what I can and cannot do?

The government places enormous emphasis on the importance of pre-application discussions and encourages all applicants to make contact with local authorities to seek advice and work together with them on development proposals.

There are a number of flaws in this appealing scenario, the most important of which is that a local authority is very unlikely to provide any meaningful positive advice. This is because it is the role of the planning officer to respond to and give a reaction to specific proposals. They will be very quick to point out that they are not planning consultants and cannot help applicants arrive at design solutions; planners really only have a modicum of design training. They may be able to indicate issues of concern, relevant considerations and potential design problems but they are working outside their remit if they give anything close to positive support.

The best one can hope for is a neutral or slightly positive reaction. This is because planning officers do not individually make decisions; they make recommendations that they do not have the authority to enforce. So any advice given is accompanied by the often unspoken caveat that any subsequent planning application will be considered on its merits subject to further opinions of the planning officer's colleagues such as their line manager, their manager and ultimately the planning committee.

It is also a simple fact that planning officers are swamped by waves of bureaucracy and generally have far too much to do – so they do not have the time, even if they have the inclination, to go beyond the minimum role of answering questions about specific proposals. The awkward position of the hapless homeowner or small developer is exacerbated by the principle that if you don't know the right questions to ask you will not get the right answers.

There are many things an individual can build without planning permission and many applications could be avoided by minor tweaks and rearrangements in size or position of a minor nature. But when confronted with a proposal they consider unacceptable, even where a minor change would avoid the need for consent at all, it is my own personal experience that some planning officers will not tell applicants that this is the case. And they have no legal obligation to do so.

Even at the most basic level some planning authorities provide no personal guidance at all beyond pointing out the relevant policies in the local plan. Increasingly, local authorities now charge a fee for pre-application advice – but the same principles apply that they will respond to suggestions and proposals in a wholly reactive manner. And, notwithstanding having paid for it this advice, it cannot be depended upon.

The best approach is therefore to consider planning officers as a resource through which you may seek to identify potential problems and as a means by which to flush out likely objections. There are a lot of very helpful planning officers who despite the limitations of their role do their best to help and it can be useful to try and get them to distinguish between their own professional opinions and their knowledge of the likely reaction of senior colleagues and of influential politicians. All these views can be different.

Is the council bound by the advice it gives me?

In a word: no. Any informal advice provided by a planning authority is given without prejudice to any formal decision they subsequently make. Because the advice is given prior to the application being submitted it will necessarily be made based on partial information, and without the benefit of all the consultation responses and without the time and effort that goes into looking at the site and considering all the issues etc. So, even when given in writing, pre-application advice absolutely cannot be relied upon.

I have personally come across instances of planning officers changing jobs and the new post-holder has taken a different view from the previous one; so the advice has then changed even before the application has been submitted, or on one occasion after it had been submitted. A paper trail of pre-application advice followed by an officer's recommendation for approval can be a material consideration for a planning inspector to take into account in a planning appeal, but it is still no guarantee.

If an authority is perceived to have led an applicant up the garden path and so behaved unreasonably this might even be a justification for the award of costs in a planning appeal, but not necessarily a decision consistent with that advice.

There are a host of situations where planning officers write letters, such as agreeing minor amendments and confirming whether planning permission is needed – but such letters have no weight in law. There is no doctrine of estoppel in planning law so even if a planning officer has written categorically to agree something (other than clearing the requirements of a condition), the planning authority are not actually legally bound by the letter.

The basic principle is that if there is a legal process available to deal with an issue then that should be used; a letter cannot be a substitute. For example if you wanted confirmation that certain changes to a house do not require planning permission then a letter confirming it might give comfort but that is not a legal substitute for a Lawful Development

Certificate which will provide a genuine legal determination comparable to a planning permission. Since the beginning of planning (in 1947) local authorities have been informally agreeing minor amendments to existing approvals in a generally pragmatic and reasonable way.

Quite recently legal precedent has determined that such letters are not binding on the authority and did not actually authorise the changes and modifications that they purport to. No doubt authorities will continue to write such letters but they are an unsatisfactory substitute in legal terms for what would really require a fresh application.

Does an extension need evidence of planning consent?

The lack of planning documentation related to a house that has obviously been extended can get solicitors in a flap and delay or even prevent the sale. Usually this is unnecessary if the extensions were built as permitted development or they were built more than four years previously.

If they were built four or more years ago then they are immune from any enforcement action that the local authority could take. This is called the four year rule which is based on the sensible principle that if something can exist for four years without the local authority taking action it can't be much of a problem. (It does not apply to alterations to listed buildings).

The formal way of confirming that a development was 'permitted development' or that it has been there for at least four years is to apply for a Lawful Development Certificate which will take at least eight weeks. In most cases this would be overkill, if the extensions are clearly more than four years old there is very unlikely to be a problem and a letter from a planning lawyer or planning consultant to that effect should be enough to overcome any jitters felt by inexperienced solicitors.

It is worth remembering that permitted development rights allow houses to be extended by a certain maximum, but once this has been reached the development rights have been used up. If the house is very old then for the purposes of permitted development it is considered to have been

'original' in 1947 so additions and alterations made before that date do not count against the available permitted development allowance.

Why can't I build a house on my paddock?

If major builders can build hundreds of houses on agricultural land why can't I built one small house on my paddock? This is a very common sentiment felt by people who own some land and cannot really understand why they can't build just one house when they seem to see nothing but high density shoeboxes being chucked up all around them.

And it's a question that goes to the heart of the basic planning policies which underpin the current system, namely that new development will only be allowed on undeveloped virgin agricultural land if it has been specifically allocated in a development plan or as a result of some special exception that is in the public interest. Special exceptions might be a dwelling needed for an existing agricultural business or for affordable housing.

The building of one nice house because you can afford it and own the land is sadly not exceptional justification. The planning system is currently obsessed with not building on agricultural land, notwithstanding the fact that only 10 per cent of our country is actually built on. The system is, as a result, orientated very much in favour of medium to large developers who use their financial muscle to buy existing houses with large gardens in leafy suburbs and carry out high density redevelopments or to buy industrial sites for redevelopment.

Alternatively they are able to promote large comprehensive developments on major allocated sites on the periphery of the larger towns and villages. This is consistent with government policy and enables local authorities to extract the maximum planning gain such as schools and highways infrastructure. The very high density housing built on these sites is a specific requirement of government policy and not just a function of the developer's greed.

In many instances developers would like to build large detached family homes in decent-sized plots to meet an undoubted market demand but current government policy, aided and abetted by the Campaign to Protect Rural England and many planners, is firmly against this. With a recommendation that houses be built at no less than 30 units to the hectare.

What is brownfield land?

This is a colloquial term used to describe the 'previously developed land' identified by the government as the most sustainable location for most new residential development. The image of brown-field land is of derelict urban sites, and although former and current industrial land and derelict land is covered this definition also includes houses in large gardens.

There can be few people who have not noticed new flats and high density housing being built where there were previously houses in large plots in pleasant low density residential areas. A point not lost on the RSPB who have raised serious concerns about the loss of wildlife habitat through the loss of such garden land.

Ironically, it would appear that many back gardens have a higher wildlife value than much of the countryside which is intensively farmed and denuded of hedges and trees. There is currently a growing recognition that this brownfield land definition is harming the attractiveness of urban areas but to restrict its meaning would imply a greater use of sacrosanct agricultural land – or the development of fewer houses. It's hard to see a vote-winner amongst these choices; development of any kind is rarely popular.

What do I do if the neighbours object?

Planning applications often bring out the worst in people: they involve new development in people's immediate home area and there is a natural resistance to change. Even though most people would like to own a nice house they are very quick to object and try and prevent the building of houses anywhere near them. So most applications for residential

development (all such applications in my experience), result in objections from neighbours and usually the relevant town or parish council. So if neighbours object it is not normally a reason to panic but it is worth finding out what they're saying and taking a view on whether there will be any political fallout that could influence the politicians against what you wish to build.

It makes sense to try and forestall objections before an application is submitted and with major schemes the government now expects developers to undertake public consultation. This consultation requirement appears to overlook the attitude of most people – which is to oppose new developments and to try and prevent them or at least reduce them as much as possible. Against this backdrop it is still worth trying to get neighbours on board by talking through their possible concerns, dealing with issues of boundaries, potential loss of privacy and access issues before submitting a planning application.

Experience has demonstrated to me that people will often claim to be satisfied and happy with the proposal and then write nasty letters to the local authority objecting anyway, so it is not a foolproof technique. But efforts made to overcome neighbours' concerns and the design responses that result can now be set out clearly in the new design and access statement and this can help explain why a particular proposal is of the form scale and character that it is.

With luck these efforts to accommodate neighbours' concerns will therefore reduce the weight given to those letters of objection by the politicians on the planning committee once they know that a serious effort has been made to work with locals whilst trying to comply with the requisite development plan and supplementary planning guidance guidelines on distances and relationships between dwellings.

Good presentation can help allay the fears of the planning committee and more reasonable people in the vicinity of a site by demonstrating clearly what the new development will look like and how it will relate in scale to the buildings that surround it.

If I lose my appeal how long is it before I can re-apply?

There are no hard and fast rules to limit when you can reapply for a revised development on a site where a scheme has been refused either locally or at appeal. The local authority does however have the power to decline to determine materially similar applications which have recently already been refused. Although this is a draconian power it does reflect a fairly reasonable principle that there is no point in applying to build something that has only recently had planning permission refused unless serious efforts are made to overcome the reasons for refusal. Once a period of two years has elapsed they cannot decline to determine but during that time it is quite likely that planning policies or the circumstances of the site could have altered.

If a proposal has been refused at appeal the inspector's comments will be taken very seriously by the local authority and become an important benchmark against which subsequent applications will be assessed. The local authority are in fact legally obliged to take into account the outcome of the decision at appeal when considering a fresh proposal. So there is no earthly point in continuing to try and get permission in the face of an appeal refusal unless the problems identified by the inspector have been overcome.

If an application is refused due to matters of detail, such as the overlooking of neighbouring properties, the geometry of access, inadequate parking, excessive height and bulk of the buildings or due to questions of aesthetics in design then a new proposal can seek to tackle and solve those particular identified problems.

However, if a negative appeal decision focuses on the issue of principle and it is clear that the proposal is unacceptable because of a direct conflict with policy in terms of the very nature of the development, it will be very difficult to overcome that refusal unless either the policy or the proposal is changed in some fundamental way. I have had experience of people who cannot take no for an answer and end up wasting years and a small fortune pursuing hopeless cases through several appeals to no avail. Sometimes this results from poor planning advice but more often it is

because they will not take the advice they are given: which is to accept defeat and move on.

How do I find out how much land is worth?

This is not really a planning question but it is one that frequently comes up whenever the prospect of development is discussed. The simple answer is the land is worth what some will pay for it, and that is usually directly related to what they can build on it and how much they can sell that development for. So in crude terms the value of the land is the value of the completed development less the build costs and the developer's profit – usually around 20 per cent.

If the site is being developed by the end user, such as a self builder, there will often be no inbuilt profit so the land value can become a very substantial proportion of the overall value of the completed scheme. The value of land can also be greatly affected in practice by the activities of whichever estate agent is instructed to sell it. In my experience many estate agents would rather sell land to local developers that they know well in order to benefit from re-sales after houses are built, rather than selling to private individuals or end users who will not bring any further selling fees to the agent.

Land can sometimes be worth far more than you expect, not because of what can be built on it but because of its importance to an adjacent development. For example if a piece of land controls an access to the development, either because the new road passes over it or because junction visibility is needed to ensure road safety, then the site may hold a ransom over its neighbour.

There are many land speculators and developers who look specifically to create and purchase ransom position is overdevelopment sites in order to extract the necessary payment. Historically, a figure of a third of the development value of the ransomed site is often agreed as the payment necessary to overcome the ransom. But ultimately, in most cases, if the land owner does not wish to release a ransom by providing the access or whatever then there is nothing a private individual can do about it other than offer money and hope a deal can be struck.

Do I need a planning consultant?

Any development proposal will ordinarily require an architect or designer to produce the plans and drawings necessary both to get planning permission and to construct the buildings. Many developers rely upon these designers and architects to deal with the planning side of the work, often with some success. But as a general rule architects and designers tend to know as much about planning as planners know about architectural design. Which is a bit, but not enough to do it.

A planning consultant can be useful in guiding the architect's designs and layouts so that they meet with the anticipated concerns and policy constraints that are likely to be encountered through the planning process. Discussions with the planning officers often benefit from having a professional on board who speaks their language, architects can sometimes be rather precious about their creations and understandably resent architecturally unqualified people (local authority planners) meddling and interfering with their designs. The planning consultant can be a useful go-between and help smooth through necessary amendments and modifications needed to actually get permission.

What does sustainable development mean?

Sustainable is the absolute buzzword in planning at the moment. The statutory purpose of planning is identified as being to 'promote sustainable development'. But understanding clearly what it means in practice, or even in theory, is nigh on impossible. There are endless different ways of interpreting how the principle of sustainability should or could be applied in any particular set of circumstances.

In the broadest sense my favourite definition of a sustainable mode of living is that we should be living off the earth's revenue not its capital. In a micro sense sustainability has become associated with all sorts of worthy green approaches to transport, lifestyles and purchases. It is a word that is bandied about in every planning document you will come across.

For those who are actually trying to build new houses, businesses or shops it is clear that planning policies are currently focused upon centralisation, but rather than use the word 'centralisation' they use the phrase 'sustainable development'.

Planners are encouraged to direct development to larger settlements, close to a wide range of services and employment with the intention that people will drive less and use alternative forms of transport more. The alternative forms of transport being, ideally, walking and cycling, then public transport such as buses or trains. The result is high density development in supposedly sustainable locations where facilities and housing are forced together in close proximity, or failing that on the edge of large towns or very large villages with the same intention.

So, in practice, assessments of sustainability tend to focus largely upon crude measurements of the distances between shops, businesses, schools and other local facilities from the proposed housing (or vice versa) and the relationship between new development and bus stops.

This approach to the centralisation of housing, employment and services – all linked by buses – has at its heart the notion of mass public transport usage of the kind found in London and in few other places in the UK. So we have a public transport based approach to land use planning in a society where the vast majority of people will, if they can possibly manage it, buy and use a car.

Because planning is highly political the sustainability agenda is essentially anti-car, notwithstanding the reality of increasing car use and declining public transport usage. The result appears to be increasing congestion, inadequate car parking provision. One might even say, 'The road to hell is paved with sustainable intentions'!

Appendix VI
GLOSSARY OF PLANNING TERMS

Jargon dances across the pages of planning documents and spews forth from the mouths of almost everyone involved in the process. This section will help you to understand exactly what they are getting at without having to find the relevant chapter in this book.

Access: Point where vehicles and/or pedestrians enter and leave a site. It is now also a term that has a broader usage in planning in the context of the new design and access statements that will accompany almost all new planning applications. To quote the very recent government advice in circular 01/06, these statements should explain how access arrangements would ensure that all new users will have equal and convenient access to buildings and spaces and the public transport network.

Accessibility: This is a word to be found in sustainability appraisals and in supporting documents that seek to demonstrate the acceptability of the site in access terms. It is increasingly used in reference to the ability of people to travel by modes of transport other than the private car; this is designed specifically to include elderly and disabled people, those with young children and those with luggage or shopping.

Adoption: The final and formal confirmation of a development plan or local development document status by a local planning authority. The adopted local plan or local development document has reached the final stage of the process and, at this point, should have the most influence on the planning

authority when it is considering planning proposals. The adopted proposals map is an important part of a local development framework or development plan and may be considered a development plan document itself as it will show proposed new housing or industrial allocations and other designated sites or restrictions like conservation areas.

Advertisement regulations: The control of outdoor advertisements and signs is governed by the Town & Country Planning (Control of Advertisements) Regulations 1992, as amended in 1994 and 1999. They specify what adverts can be put up without consent and those that need it. The freedoms encompassed by the current advert regs, as they are known, are often not fully appreciated or exploited by shop owners and other commercial operators.

Affordable housing: See social housing.

Aftercare: The programme of works required to complete a minerals working or waste disposal site so that an alternative use of the land is possible, such as agriculture, nature conservation or leisure uses. Aftercare proposals normally include an ongoing maintenance programme.

Aggregates: Sand, gravel, crushed rock and other bulk materials used by the construction industry.

Agricultural worker's dwelling: This is sometimes called an 'ag tag' or agricultural tie. A dwelling that is subject to a planning condition or legal agreement limiting its occupation to someone employed, or was last employed, in agriculture, forestry or other appropriate rural employment. Removing an agricultural worker's dwelling normally requires the applicant to demonstrate there is no longer any realistic demand in the area for a dwelling to house such a worker.

Ambient noise: When used in the context of a noise survey this refers to the existing background noise level (such as road noise) against which other unusual or nuisance noise (like proposed or existing industrial use) will be assessed.

Amenity: A word much loved by planners; an all embracing description of virtually anything that is beneficial or desirable in terms of the physical or

visual environment. It is a word used endlessly in planning policies to refer to anything that makes a positive contribution to the overall character or enjoyment of an area. For example, privacy, sunlight, a private garden area, open land, trees, historic buildings and the inter-relationship between them.

Amenity area or green-space: The first phrase tends to mean private garden the second refers to a public open space that makes a positive contribution to the appearance of an area and adds to the quality of the lives of people within the locality.

Ancillary use: A subsidiary or secondary use or operation closely associated with the main use of a building or piece of land. For example, the offices required in association with a light industrial use. It is possible to have some ancillary uses that are quite different to the main authorised use of a building without creating the need for a change of use application. For example, it is possible to work from home as an ancillary activity to living there. Providing that the commercial use always remains ancillary to the residential use no planning permission is required.

Ancient woodland: Woodland that is believed to have existed from at least medieval times. Often a haven for wildlife and its existence will often be indicated on local plan proposals maps.

Annual monitoring report: A report that is submitted annually to the government by local planning authorities or regional planning bodies to describe and assess the progress of creating and implementing a local development framework. This report has important implications for monitoring the success of the council's housing policies. If they are not able to provide a deliverable five-year housing land supply, it may indicate the need to review this part of the local development framework, so the AMR will be of interest to more than just the government.

Appeal: If an application for planning permission is refused, or an enforcement notice is issued against a site within the statutory time period of eight or 13 weeks, it is possible to lodge an appeal. This can take one of three forms; written representations, informal hearing or public inquiry.

Approved documents: Technical guidance produced by the government that demonstrates how compliance with building regulations can be achieved.

Approved inspectors: Private bodies approved by the Construction Industry Council who can certify that work is in compliance with the building regulations as an alternative to local authority building control.

Archaeological assessment/evaluation/watching brief: If a planning application is in a location, or includes a building with potential above or below ground archaeological interest, a planning condition can be imposed to require an archaeological evaluation, or watching brief. This monitors any archaeological finds that appear during the development process. If the location of the development is such that important archaeological remains could genuinely limit or constrain the development of the site, a pre-determination archaeological evaluation may be required. This means that the planning authority resolve to grant permission but don't actually issue the permission notice until a programme of works has been agreed and the subsequent field evaluation has taken place. If the pre-determination evaluation reveals interesting archaeology, then a full-scale excavation may be required before development commences and the scheme may need to be modified to protect archaeological remains. Such archaeological investigations can be very expensive and time-consuming but archaeological conditions are not always such a problem. They can be limited to a desk-based assessment or a field assessment involving a ground survey and small-scale pits, or trial trenching, carried out by professionally qualified archaeologists. All paid for, of course, by the applicant. Remember, archaeological finds will usually belong to the landowner, not to the bunch of private archaeological consultants who are paid to dig them up or the local authority who have insisted on it.

Area action plan: A type of development plan document focused on a specific location or an area. See local development framework.
Area of outstanding natural beauty (AONB): A national statutory landscape designation, the primary purpose of which is to conserve and enhance natural beauty of the area. This designation has the same protective power as National Park status. AONB are designated by the countryside agency.

Areas of special control of advertisements: Give stricter control over advertisements in areas where the council considers there is justification because of scenic, historical, architectural or cultural features.

Article Four direction: A power under the Town & Country Planning (General Development) Order 1995 allowing a council to limit or remove the permitted development rights of existing properties and land. Compensation can be payable by the local authority to the property owner for the reduced property value resulting from an article four direction.

Article 14 direction: A holding direction (in the form of a letter) issued by the government stating that a local planning authority cannot grant planning permission for a particular proposal until further notice. This enables the government to decide whether or not to call in a particular application for their determination which will involve a public inquiry.

Backland development: Development of 'landlocked' sites behind existing buildings, such as rear gardens and private open space, usually within predominantly residential areas. Such sites often have no street frontages and access is created either by knocking down an existing dwelling or by squeezing it in between existing properties. Such development used to be frowned upon by planners. But since the government's strong emphasis on the development of previously developed land, including back gardens, it is increasingly being accepted as a way of enabling the more efficient and intensive development of land in urban areas.

Best and most versatile agricultural land: Land identified by the Department for Environment, Food and Rural Affairs (DEFRA) as falling within classification grades 1, 2 or 3a, based on the physical characteristics of the land and the limits these impose upon its agricultural uses.

Best value: The name given to a whole raft of government-inspired targets and programme requirements used by local authorities to manage their performance against a large number of government targets. These targets are aimed at the authority's performance as measured by its best value performance indicators. The eight and 13-week statutory periods are just two of the many best value performance indicators.

Betterment: A development land tax that is intended to extract some of the development value of land. Increasingly seen as a possible way of funding local infrastructure and soon to take the name of Planning Gain Supplement.

Biodiversity: The variety of plants, animals and other living things in a particular area or region. It encompasses habitat diversity, species diversity and genetic diversity.

Biodiversity action plan: A local area strategy aimed at conserving and enhancing biological diversity produced by local authorities, often in association with planning policy documents and other environmental initiatives.

Biomass: Living matter within an environmental area. For example: plant material, vegetation or agricultural waste used as a fuel or energy source.

Blight: In essence, a function of uncertainty often associated with long-term planning proposals that fail to materialise. Planning blight prevents people from planning the future of their properties, investing money with security and in taking business decisions. Blight has a depressing effect on the value and desirability of an area by deterring potential investment at the same time as making properties more difficult to sell. It may have the effect of causing landowners to hold onto properties in the belief that their forthcoming planning proposal will make them more valuable but in the meantime the uncertainty acts against short or medium term investment.

Borrow pit: A temporary mineral working to supply material for a specific construction project.

Breach of conditions notice: A formal notice served by a local planning authority where it suspects that a planning condition linked to a planning permission has been breached. Failure to comply with conditions can be a serious offence and result in prosecution, although most local authorities only take it that far if they fail to solve the problem through dialogue.

Brief/planning brief: A planning brief can include site-specific development briefs, design briefs, development frameworks and master plans that seek to guide and influence the shape of future development. It is not uncommon for the production of development briefs to be part of major housing allocations and to be appended to development plan documents.

Bring systems (public recycling facilities): Recycling schemes where the public

delivers their recyclables to a central collection point, such as those in supermarket car parks, for bottles and cans.

Brownfield land: Also described as previously developed land but to have slightly different meanings. The government defines 'previously-developed land' quite specifically as land which is, or was, occupied by a permanent structure (excluding agricultural or forestry buildings) and associated fixed-surface infrastructure. The definition covers the curtilage of the development. Planning Policy Statement 3 (Housing) has a detailed definition. Many local authorities and the public refer to brownfield sites more loosely with reference to any land or premises that has previously been used or developed, including land that is vacant, derelict or contaminated.

Buffer zone: An area of land separating certain types of development from adjoining sensitive land uses. Often used in relation to minerals and/or waste development.

Building preservation notice: Temporary listed building status normally granted for six months. During this time the Secretary of State will consider whether the building should be protected by listed building status. The building should be of special historic or architectural interest and be in danger of demolition or alteration harmful to the character of the building.

Building notice: A notice in prescribed form given to the local authority under Regulation 12(2)(a) and 13 of the building regulations informing the authority of proposed work. Building notices contain a limited amount of information concerning building proposals and enable work to be carried out without preparing detailed plans. See Chapter 11.

Buildings at Risk Register: A national schedule of listed buildings that are considered by English Heritage to be under threat, due to neglect, poor repair, blight or proposed developments; or simply at risk of being lost owing to their dilapidated condition. The list is updated annually.

Commission for Architecture and the Built Environment (CABE): A fairly recent public body acting as a champion of good design in England. It has a website and issues good practice guides aimed at stimulating what it considers

to be good design. CABE expects to be consulted on major development schemes. Call-in or called-in planning application: The relevant minister can 'call in' certain planning applications for his or her own determination in cases where the local authorities propose to approve a development, e.g. where it may have wider effects beyond the immediate locality, significant regional or national controversy, or potential conflict with national policy. These will then be subject to a public inquiry presided over by a planning inspector who will make recommendation to the government who then takes the final decision.

Certificate of Immunity from listing: This can be applied for to give security against spot listing or the issuing of a building preservation notice for a period of five years. This certificate can only be granted when a property is subject to a planning application or recent permission.

Change of use: The Town & Country Planning Act, 1990, defines development as building and other similar operations, including changes of use of property and land. Planning permission is, therefore, required for a material change of use from one use class to the other. A planning application is also not required for changes of use that are permitted development. See also Use Classes Order

Chief planning officer: The head planning officer at a local authority. Often has very little to do with the day-to-day work of planning and is increasingly embroiled in the political side of departmental management, focusing upon targets and customer care initiatives and dealing with particularly intransigent and high-profile objectors.

Circular advice: Government publications that set out procedural matters and guidance on the implementation of new polices, statutory changes and requirements. Government circulars are important as a constituent of planning policy. What they say will be taken very seriously by the local authority and appeal inspectors.

Claw-back: often used to describe a legal covenant on land, which needs to be removed before the site can be developed. Such covenants are designed to enable former owners to claw back money arising from the uplift in value generated by a new or revised planning permission. Such covenants are sometimes described as ransoms.

Coalescence: The expansion and eventual merging of separate towns or villages. It is not infrequent to see instances of towns that have swallowed up the villages that used to surround them. The use of green belt designation around major towns was created to prevent it and remains the strongest planning tool to inhibit the coalescence. The prevention of coalescence was one of the main aims of the town planning system when first introduced.

Commitments (or committed development): A development plan term used to describe land with a current planning permission or land that has been formally allocated for development in an adopted development plan. The extent of housing commitments related to housing completions (the properties that have been built) will influence the amount of land that needs to be found for new housing development in a local authority area. PPS 3 requires local authorities to be able to show a deliverable five year land supply.

Completion certificate: Based on the evidence available, this declares that the completed work described complies with the building regulations.

Community forest: A large area of land within which it is hoped that, eventually, there will be a wooded landscape - created, promoted and managed by a partnership of local authorities, national agencies and private, voluntary and community organisations with the aim of supporting employment, recreation, education and wildlife.

Community strategy: A strategy prepared by each local authority intended to improve local quality of life; covering a vast array of issues including things over which the local planning authority has absolutely no control.

Commmuted payment: Agreement may be reached whereby a developer pays for provision off site rather than as part of a scheme. For example instead of providing the full amount of parking spaces required on a site, the developer provides only limited on-site spaces plus cash. Commuted payments are implemented by the Section 106 Agreement mechanism and can relate to the provision of public car parking spaces, public transport, public open space, affordable housing, educational contributions etc.

Compulsory purchase order (CPO): An order issued by the government or a local authority to acquire land or buildings for public interest purposes. For example, to facilitate land assembly for the construction of a major road or the redevelopment of certain brownfield sites. The powers available to local authorities are set out in Government Circular 06/04.

Conditions of planning permission: May be imposed to help make a proposed development comply with planning policies. For example, requiring a landscaping scheme to be planted, or a certain building material to be used, or specified visibility splays provided at the access. According to government circular 11/95 conditions must be:
■ Necessary
■ Relevant to planning
■ Relevant to the development
■ Enforceable
■ Precise
■ Reasonable in all other aspects

It is possible to make a planning application to relax (i.e. remove or vary the terms of) a condition or to appeal against the imposition of a condition, using the same appeal process as used to appeal against a planning refusal before the development has been commenced.

Conditions precedent. See Chapter 2

Conservation area: An area designated under the Town & Country Planning (Listed Buildings and Conservation Areas) Act, 1990 as possessing special architectural or historic interest. The council has a duty to preserve or enhance the character and appearance of these areas.

Conservation area character appraisal: A published document defining the special architectural or historic interest that warranted the area being designated, it can be useful in trying to argue a case in favour of a development.

Conservation area consent: Under the planning (Listed Buildings & Conservation Areas) Act 1990, consent is required to carry out the demolition of buildings and structures in conservation areas. See Chapter 4.

Contaminated land: Land that has been polluted and contains waste material that requires remediation before development can take place. The Environment Agency's definition of waste is very wide so most former industrial land is likely to contain some contamination, however limited.

Controlled waste: Waste that requires a special licence for its treatment or disposal.

Conversions: Generally means the physical work necessary to change the use of a building from one use to another. Can also mean the sub-division of residential properties into self-contained flats or maisonettes.

County structure plan: This is a now superseded county-wide set of general planning policies within which the more detailed district and borough planning policies must conform. No longer being produced – for the new system see Chapter 3.

Core strategy: See Chapter 3

County council: The local authority that is becoming increasingly irrelevant in planning terms as its strategic policy making function has been taken away by the regional spatial strategies produced by unelected regional planning bodies. Counties are still usually responsible for waste and minerals planning functions in non-unitary, and non-national park, local authority areas. A county council may still provide advice on strategic planning issues to the regional planning body. Previously, county councils were responsible for the creation of the structure plan, which provided the strategic background to the creation of local plans within the county area. This has now been replaced with the relationship between the local development framework of the district and borough level and the regional planning policies.

Consultation: This takes place in relation to all planning applications in the form of statutory and non-strategy consultations. The application follows a set procedure as it works its way through the planning department and this includes a consultation period of 21 days. Once this period has expired, local authority will be at liberty to determine the proposal. Delays can occur when important organisations, like a highway authority or highways agency or

environment agency, are slow in providing meaningful responses, (of course an acknowledgement or request for further information is enough to satisfy statutory targets). The government is keen on the idea of consultation for assessing public opinion about a plan or major development proposal, or in the case of a planning application, the means of obtaining the views of affected neighbours or others. It is anticipated that developers will work with stakeholders during the consultation process. To many people in the industry the whole consultation exercise is fraught with delays and fruitless expense as in many cases planning applications are routinely opposed as unnecessary local development and unwelcome change by the relevant existing local populace. Local consultations serve to demonstrate how most people can be relied upon to object to new development as a matter of principle.

Curtain walling: A non-load-bearing wall applied to exterior elevations of a framed structure using metal, glass or thin masonry units to form the external finish to a building.

Curtilage: Land attached to a house that forms one distinct area of enclosure. The curtilage of a dwelling house is of course critical to establishing what can be classified as previously developed land for the purposes of potential redevelopment. Also permitted development rights will only be available to land that is legally defined as curtilage. The definition of what is, and is not, curtilage has been subject to numerous planning debates and some planning law precedent. With regard to listed buildings, defining the curtilage may be important in determining, for example, whether outbuildings and walls are included along with the main house in the statutory listing.

Delegated powers: Legal powers conferred to designated planning officers by the planning committee, which enables those planning officers to take planning decisions on specified planning matters on behalf of the council. So individual officers may have the power to grant or refuse permission behind closed doors without any public hearing, even though there may be objections or letters or support.

Demand responsive transport: A local transport service that responds to specific requests, operating in a similar way to a taxi service. Known in some areas as dial-a-ride or community buses.

Density: In the case of residential development, this is a measurement of either the number of habitable rooms per hectare or the number of dwellings per hectare.

Department for Communities and Local Government (DCLG): The successor department to the Office of the Deputy Prime Minister (ODPM). The web site contains a lot of relevant planning policy information.

Departure (to the development plan): A proposed development that is significantly contrary to the adopted development plan such that it would threaten to undermine and run contrary to its expressed purpose, but for which the local planning authority proposes to grant planning permission. Most advertised departures are actually too minor to be treated as such and the relevant regional government body does not step in.

Design Commission for Wales (DCFW): A government organisation funded by the National Assembly for Wales. DCFW's stated purpose is like that of the English version, CABE; to promote what they consider to be high standards of architecture, landscape and urban design in Wales and, of course, promote the importance of their opinions as to what constitutes good quality in the built environment.

Design guide: Produced by local authorities as supplementary planning guidance to help guide the appearance and neighbourliness of proposed new developments. They tend to cover issues like privacy distances, amenity space standards, parking standards plus an indication of what the authority thinks defines local distinctiveness in their area. Sometimes local authorities have produced area character appraisals, which add a further level of detailed design guidance specific to a few streets. Ultimately, of course, what is considered to be in character or out of keeping is just as subjective as ever, beauty being in the eye of the beholder etc. In my view design guides tend to give the local authority more influence and enable them to justify refusals without really giving a designer more confidence about what might actually be allowed.

Design and access statement: The requirement for this is set out fully in circular 01/06. See Chapter 8.

Detailed application/full application: A planning application that seeks permission for a particular development proposal, with no detailed matters reserved for later planning approval. This kind of application includes full detailed drawings of exactly

what is proposed. The alternative is an Outline Application. See Chapter 2

Development brief: A prescriptive list of design and planning gain requirements that a local authority wants to impose upon a particular site or area allocated for development. Sometimes produced in association with the proposed developer, it can be a requirement of pre-application discussions on a major site.

Development control: Usual name given to the local authority department that deals specifically with planning applications. Can often be interpreted to mean development prevention!

Development plan: The planning policy framework first introduced by the Town & Country Planning Act 1947 and recently renamed and rearranged with more power concentrated into the hands of central government. See Chapter 3

Development plan documents (DPDs): Outline the key development goals of the local development framework. See Chapter 3

Disabled access: Requirements regulated by the Disability Discrimination Act 1995 and .

Dwelling: A self-contained residential unit occupied either by a person or group of people living together as a family, or by not more than six residents living together as a single household. A dwelling may be a house, bungalow, flat or maisonette.

Elevation: A drawing representing one side of a building, referred to as the north, east, south or west elevation of the building depending upon which way it faces.

Employment land availability: The local authority's assessment of the total amount of land in an area available for industrial and business use, perhaps with planning permission and awaiting development.

Enforcement action: Procedures undertaken by a local planning authority to enforce compliance with planning law so that a building is built in accordance

with approved plans. That a planning condition is complied with or that an unauthorised activity or development is either stopped or controlled through the grant of planning permission. Enforcement action is discretionary, the planning authority does not have to take action. If a proposal is unlawful then requesting a planning application is a reasonable response. If such an application for retrospective permission is submitted, the authority cannot penalise the applicant just because it was built without permission, regardless of how much the elected councilors or angry locals would like them to.

Enforcement notice: A formal legal notice served by a local planning authority that sets out the actions necessary to bring a development back into accordance with a planning permission, or permitted development rights, or to put right work or stop or modify an activity that has been undertaken or is continuing without planning permission. An enforcement notice can be appealed against in the same way as a planning refusal or planning conditions. See Chapter 12.

English Nature: Now called Natural England. Government-funded organisation that advises local authorities on nature conservation issues in England.

Environment Agency: Known as the EA (formerly the National Rivers Authority – NRA) this government body is responsible for all things to do with flooding, waste management, licensing and disposal and with contaminated land. They will be consulted on any development involving a contaminated site or land in flood plain or land liable to flood. It is a good idea to sort out all potential drainage, land remediation or flooding issues with them before submitting a planning application, which could involve them. It is probable that there will not be enough time during the processing of the application to sort these things out with the EA and you will have to withdraw and start again.

Environmental Assessment/Environmental Statement: Required under the Town & Country Planning (Environmental Impact Assessment) Regulations 1999, the assessment is the name given to the all encompassing analysis that is needed to produce an environmental statement (ES). This is a major additional legal requirement that must accompany a planning application for major developments, and or those that are anticipated as having significant environmental effects. There are a range of pre-established thresholds and guidelines that are used to determine whether a particular application will

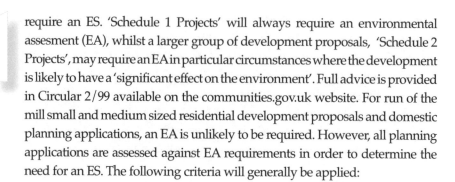

require an ES. 'Schedule 1 Projects' will always require an environmental assesment (EA), whilst a larger group of development proposals, 'Schedule 2 Projects', may require an EA in particular circumstances where the development is likely to have a 'significant effect on the environment'. Full advice is provided in Circular 2/99 available on the communities.gov.uk website. For run of the mill small and medium sized residential development proposals and domestic planning applications, an EA is unlikely to be required. However, all planning applications are assessed against EA requirements in order to determine the need for an ES. The following criteria will generally be applied:

■ Is the project a major scheme of more than local importance?
■ Is the project taking place in a particularly sensitive area [Conservation Area, National Park, S.S.S.I.], which would give rise, as a result, to significant effects upon the environment?
■ Is the proposal likely to give rise to complex or adverse effects, such as pollutant discharge etc?

If you submit a major scheme, it may seem temping to let them tell you if an EA is needed rather than submitting a prior request for a screening opinion, which is the correct way of determining whether an EA is needed. But there is one big disadvantage to this; the applicant then becomes responsible for all the consultations required, not the local authority. Generally speaking, environmental assessments, and the resultant statements, are heaven for a wide range of specialist consultants and cost tens of thousands of pounds. Applications that are accompanied by an EA have an extended statutory period of 16 weeks to give the local authority more time, but I doubt if one has ever been processed that quickly.

Fenestration: Term used to describe the arrangement, style and number of windows in a building.

Flood plain: A broad term used to describe many different kinds of areas that are liable to flood. The Environment Agency has large scale computer-based flood plain maps that are indicative and may not be totally accurate. It is an important planning consideration as development is generally resisted in such areas even if mitigation measures can be undertaken.

Flood risk assessment: This will be required as part of a planning application anywhere near a watercourse or floodplain. They can vary in scale and complexity and it is important not to use a sledgehammer to crack a nut when dealing with remote, but theoretically possible, flooding issues. Major developments in floodplains will need very expensive and complex flood risk assessments, minor schemes can be simpler and much less costly.

Full plans application (building regulations): See Chapter 11

General permitted development order: Regulations, which set out the law in relation to permitted development, See Appendix I

Green belt: Not to be confused with the term greenfield or with simple open countryside. This is a formal national designation attached to specific areas of land around certain cities and large built-up areas, which aims to keep this land permanently open and undeveloped. Any development that does not fall within a small defined group of exceptions, such as agricultural buildings, is termed inappropriate development. Green belt is the closest thing in planning to a large rubber stamp with 'NO' on it. Having said this, there are rumbles about the need to release green belt land for much needed housing, as it is quite often unattractive, ecologically barren, neglected and privately owned urban fringe whose development would be no loss to the world. However, it's potentially political suicide because of the highly emotive use of what is a largely misunderstood word.

Greenfield land: Land (usually farmland) that has not previously been developed.

Groundwater: Underground water, sometimes within strata known as aquifers.

Habitable rooms: Sometimes used to measure density, often an important consideration when determining whether there is overlooking or harm to the residential amenities of a dwelling. Habitable rooms tend to be separate living rooms, bedrooms and kitchens with a floor area of 13 square meters or more. Generally any room used, or intended to be used, for cooking, living, eating or sleeping purposes could be described as habitable. Enclosed spaces such as

bathrooms, toilets, cupboards, landings, hallways, corridors, laundries, utility rooms, lobbies and recesses are not included.

Hazardous waste: Wastes that have the potential to cause harm to human health or the environment.

High court challenge: The only way of challenging a planning appeal decision is by a high court challenge. It is not possible to question the planning merits, as it must be a challenge on a point of law. For example, failure to take into account certain key material considerations, or the application of the wrong planning policy, or fundamental errors in the process. If a high court challenge against a planning appeal decision is successful, that decision will be quashed and the appeal determined afresh by a different planning inspector. The actual result may end up being the same, so winning in the high court may not actually change much.

High hedges: These are dealt with under Part 8 of the Anti-Social Behaviour Act. Provided that a person has tried all other avenues for resolving a neighbouring hedge dispute, the complaint may be taken to the local authority (unitary, district or borough council). They will charge a potentially large amount to get involved. The role of the local authority is quite clear; it is to adjudicate on whether – to quote the Act – 'the hedge is adversely affecting the complainant's reasonable enjoyment of their property'. In doing so, the authority must take account of all relevant factors and must strike a balance between the competing interests of the complainant and hedge owner, as well as the interests of the wider community.

If they consider the circumstances justify it, the local authority will issue a formal notice to the hedge owner, which will set out what they must do to the hedge to remedy the problem and when by. Failure to carry out the works required by the authority is an offence which, on prosecution, could lead to a fine of up to £1,000.

Highway: A crucial word that sometimes suffers from a troublesome ambiguity; it can mean different things depending upon the context. Generally it means a publicly maintained road (together with footways and verges) over which the public have the right to pass. It can also mean any road or access,

whether privately owned or not, across which the general public have the right to pass.

Highways Agency: An executive agency of the Department of Transport, responsible for operating, maintaining and improving the strategic road network of England.

Historic park and garden: A park or garden of special historic interest. Graded like a listed building: I (highest quality), II* or II. Designated by English Heritage and equivalents in Scotland and Wales. See Appendix 2

House in multiple occupation (HMO): A single dwelling occupied by more than one household as bed-sits or almost self-contained accommodation, usually with some sharing of amenities such as bathrooms and toilets.

Household: Is about people. One person living alone, or a group of people (who may, or may not be, related) living at the same address with common housekeeping, sharing at least one meal a day, or occupying a common living or sitting room is described as a household. (See also Dwelling).

Human Rights Act: The Human Rights Act 1998 incorporated provisions of the European Convention on Human Rights (ECHR) into UK law. The specific Articles of the ECHR, relevant to planning, include Article 6 (right to a fair and public hearing), Article 8 (right to respect for private and family life, home and correspondence), Article 14 (prohibition of discrimination) and Article 1 of Protocol 1 (right to peaceful enjoyment of possessions and protection of property).

Independent Examination in Public (EiP): The phrase used to describe the forum in which a planning inspector publicly examines and debates the key elements of the local development framework. Such development plan documents or statements of community involvement. The inspector then issues a binding report. The examination process is less confrontational and formal than the previous public inquiry format; some say less thorough, less rigorous and less testing of the evidence, all rather important issues given the vital nature of the inspector's report for all concerned.

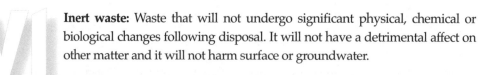

Inert waste: Waste that will not undergo significant physical, chemical or biological changes following disposal. It will not have a detrimental affect on other matter and it will not harm surface or groundwater.

Infill development: A much used phrase meaning slotting a house into an otherwise continuous built up road frontage. Generally considered acceptable within built up areas as it can be done without harming their general appearance.

Informal hearing: See Chapter 10

Inspector's report: A report issued by a planning inspector following an appeal, or the independent examination of a development plan or an other planning inquiry.

Issues, options and preferred options: Phrases used to denote the rigmarole of 'pre-submission' consultation stages. These form part of the local development framework and have the intention of achieving some measure of local consensus in relation to the policies and proposals that form the meat of the development plan documents that will be submitted to the government for independent examination by a planning inspector in an independent Examination in Public (EiP).

Key worker housing: The government's definition of key workers includes those groups eligible for the Housing Corporation funded Key Worker Living programme and others employed within the public sector (ie outside of this programme) identified by the Regional Housing Board, for assistance. The phrase usually refers to housing aimed at workers in public services where there are serious recruitment and retention problems.

Landbank: This phrase is used in different ways by different people. Many developers refer to it as land they own that has yet to get planning permission. It may also be used to mean land with planning permission but where development has yet to take place. Those who are opposed to the release of new land for housing often use the phrase incorrectly and assume that all the land that developers have control of has planning permission and is capable of development.

Lawful development certificate (LDC): A certificate issued by a local planning authority, on application, stating that an existing (LDC 191) or proposed use (LDC 192), or other forms of development, can be considered as lawful for planning purposes. It may be applied for to confirm that a proposal is permitted development or that a current unauthorised use has been operating long enough, and without a break, to render it immune from planning enforcement. A lawful development certificate is the only legally binding way, short of submitting a planning application, to establish whether or not planning permission is required for a particular existing or proposed use of development. A letter from the local authority indicating that planning permission is not required has no validity in law. See Chapter 12.

Legibility (in terms of settlement patterns): An urban design term used to denote an area, which has a strong sense of local identity that is easy to navigate mentally; the opposite of an estate full of identical cul-de-sacs where you immediately feel lost. Most historic towns are intrinsically legible as they have evolved over time with numerous unique combinations of elements and landmark buildings. Many modern estates are not.

Limits of development (or Settlement boundaries): Limits of development are usually shown on a development plan proposals map as areas within which proposals for new development may be acceptable, subject to compliance with the relevant development plan policies. Development limits are aimed at preventing the enlargement of a settlement into the surrounding countryside.

Listed buildings: See Appendix II

Local agenda 21: A comprehensive action strategy prepared by local authorities to help achieve sustainable development.

Local development documents (LDDs): See Chapter 3.

Local development framework (LDF): See Chapter 3.

Local development order (LDO): See Chapter 3.

Local development scheme (LDS): See Chapter 3.

Local listing (or building of local importance): A building considered to be historically important locally, whether for its contribution to a street or in its own right, but is not worthy of genuine listed building status and therefore has no equivalent statutory protection.

Local plan: See Chapter 3.

Local planning authority: The local authority or council that is empowered by law to exercise planning functions. Normally the unitary authority, local borough or district council; the National Parks and the Broads authority are also local planning authorities. County councils are the usual planning authorities for waste and minerals matters. Parish councils are not planning authorities even though they often have planning sub committees.

London plan: The Mayor of London is responsible for producing a spatial development strategy for the capital. This replaces RPG3 the previous strategic planning guidance for London that was issued by the Secretary of State.

Maisonette: A flat with more than one level.

Mast-sharing: Circumstances in which telecommunication operators are sharing an antenna mast or a site, in theory helping to reduce visual impact. It is actively encouraged by the government and operators must demonstrate that they have seriously considered this option.

Material consideration: The definition of material considerations could take up the whole book. In effect anything that effects, or is affected by, the development of land has the capacity in certain circumstances to be a material consideration. Perhaps 'relevant matter' might be a better phrase. Planning lawyers always seem very reluctant to discard almost anything as potentially material, because of greater importance is the weight accorded to it by the decision maker in reaching their decision.

Metropolitan open land: Open land of strategic significance, which contributes to the structure or character of a borough. In terms of protection from development this is only one step down from green belt designation.

Mixed use (or mixed use development): This just means a development that is not solely housing, leisure or employment. In an ideal world, mixed use developments are seen as a sustainable kind of approach in which people can live and work in close proximity so reducing the need to travel.

National Land Use Database: A government database to providing information on the amount of previously developed land (and buildings) with potential for future development, but not necessarily available as such.

National Park: National statutory designation whose purpose is to conserve and enhance the natural beauty, wildlife and cultural heritage of the area. National Park authorities are the local planning authorities for that area.
Net site area: The area contained within the boundaries of an application site, as defined by the red line on the planning application but excluding significant areas of landscaping or open space and roads. See Chapter 3.

Noise exposure category: In terms of planning guidance, when assessing a proposal for residential development near to a source of noise, planning authorities use noise exposure categories to help consider the effects. These are set out in PPG 24.

Outline application: See Chapter 8.

Overbearing: A highly subjective term used to describe the impact of a development or building on its surroundings, particularly a neighbouring property, in terms of its scale, massing and general dominating effect. Beloved of planning officers who want to refuse a domestic scale development that complies with all the set criteria.

Overburden: Soil and other material that overlays a mineral deposit and which has to be excavated and either tipped or stockpiled to gain access to the underlying mineral.

Overdevelopment: A favourite phrase used by planning committees and planning officers to describe schemes where they believe there is too much development. In the same way as something being out of character with the area is a very subjective judgment. The phrase can also be used where planners and objectors can't think of anything more precise or specific to refuse something on.

Overlooking: A term used to describe the loss of privacy that results from permitting a new development, which either causes, or suffers from, overlooking by neighbours. Most local authorities have standard rules of thumb to measure overlooking set out in their supplementary planning guidance. A distance of 21m between facing first-floor windows to habitable rooms is normally considered a minimum but this can be reduced where the relationship is at an angle or where non-habitable rooms are involved.

Overshadowing: The effect of a development or building on the amount of natural light enjoyed by a neighbouring property. Often used by planners as a reason for refusing what they consider to be developments that harm residential amenities. Rarely worked out very scientifically, it is often a subjective assessment assisted by rules of thumb such as the 45 degree rule (see Chapter 4). Recent case law suggests that right to light issues may come into play for objectors even where planners have judged a scheme to be acceptable in those terms.

Party Wall Act 1996: A non-planning, compulsory legal framework for preventing and resolving disputes between neighbouring owners in respect of party walls and other similar matters.

Permitted development: See Appendix I.

Planning aid: Planning aid provides free and independent advice and support to community groups and individuals who are unable/unwilling to employ a planning consultant.

Planning committee: Comprises locally elected councillors, with the relevant local political parties represented in proportion to the political make up of the council overall. The chairman and vice-chairman are elected by the controlling group on the committee. The committee will determine planning applications and often the agreement of policy drafting on behalf of the council and deal with enforcement matters. The government's target is that 90 per cent of all applications do not go to a planning committee but are dealt with by officers using delegated powers.

Planning condition: Conditions attached to a planning permission. For example, designated materials must be used for the build. See Chapter 2.

Planning delivery grant: PDG payments made to councils in reward to improving their planning performance. This includes dealing with applications in accordance with the set targets. Hence the inflexibility and unreasonableness shown by planning authorities when applicants try to negotiate and resolve problems on current applications.

Planning gain: An expression commonly used for the product of planning obligations (an agreement under Section 106 of the Town & Country Planning Act 1990 regarding the use of a development or land.) An obligation may be made by agreement between an applicant for planning permission and the council, or by a unilateral undertaking by the applicant. It is used to obtain works or financial contributions (commuted sums) necessary to help the local community infrastructure or local environment or road system to accommodate the environmental or social impact of a development. Planning gain contributions are often required towards road schemes and off-site highway works needed to accommodate additional traffic. Contributions may also be paid towards community centres, leisure and recreation facilities, social housing and other forms of community infrastructure that are necessary to support major new development proposals.

Planning gain is not intended as a mechanism to buy planning permission by offering excessive sweeteners. The government is currently proposing a planning gain supplement which, is in effect a development land tax. A debate currently rages as to what proportion of that tax would actually find its way into the hands of the local authority and how much would simply be siphoned off to the Treasury. At the time of writing the issue of planning gain supplement is unresolved.

Planning Inspectorate: An executive agency of the government, responsible for:
■ The processing of planning and enforcement appeals
■ Holding inquiries into local development plans
■ Listed building consent appeals
■ Advertisement appeals

■ Reporting on planning applications called in for decision by the department of Communities and Local Government or in Wales with the National Assembly for Wales

■ Examinations of development plan documents and statements of community involvement

■ Various compulsory purchase orders and rights of way cases. Cases arising from the Environmental Protection and Water Acts and the Transport and Works Act and other highways legislation are also dealt with.

Planning obligations and agreements: See Section 106 Agreement.

Planning panel or Planning sub-committee: Sometimes used by local authorities as a sub group of the main planning committee. These sub groups are created for the purpose of conducting a site visit or meeting concerning a specific planning application. This enables the applicants to explain their proposals and for the panel to ask questions. Unlike a normal committee meeting, the public may also be able to ask questions. The application will then be determined in formal session by the full planning committee.

Planning permission: Formal written approval granted by a local council or by the Planning Inspectorate following an appeal. Normally granted subject to specific time limits and other conditions. Can be in the form of an outline or full detailed application. A reserved matters submission that follows an outline is not technically a separate planning permission

Planning portal (www.planningportal.gov.uk): A national website sponsored by the government with the probable goal of eventual privatisation. It's aimed at members of the public, local planning authorities and commercial planning consultants, as an electronic gateway to planning information and services provided by both national and local government.

Previously developed land (PDL): See Brownfield land

Prior approval: A procedure in which permission is deemed to have been granted if the local planning authority has not responded to a formal notification within a set time period. Usually relates to telecommunication and agricultural developments.

Public art: Sometimes planning policies require financial contributions to physical works of public art to be erected as part of new major developments. They are supposed to add to good urban design, sense of place and, I guess, civic pride. Very odd really.

Public Inquiry: A formal quasi-judicial hearing presided over by a planning inspector, used to determine major planning matters such as an application called in by the Secretary of State or a major planning appeal. They are highly formal in character and involve representation by barristers on both sides with the cross-examination of witnesses. Public inquiries tend to be expensive to participate in and extremely time-consuming. See Chapter 10.

Public open space: Self explanatory. Usually areas of public open space are required as part of any sizeable housing development, managed either by parish councils or resident associations set up by the developers. Public open space is one element of planning gain that may also include a financial sum for its on-going maintenance. It is generally provided for the specific purpose of public access and outdoor use. All land and areas of public value, including significant landscaped areas, playing fields etc, which can offer opportunities for sport and recreation or can also act as a visual amenity and a haven for wildlife and may loosely be described as public open space.

Public realm: The parts of a village, town or city that are available, regardless of ownership, for everyone to use.

Public right of way: A public right of way is a highway over which the public has a legal right of access.

Ramsar sites: Sites designated under the European Ramsar Convention to protect wetlands that are of international importance, particularly as waterfowl habitats.

Reasoned justification: This is the name given to the supporting text in a development plan or local development document that explains and justifies the policies found therein.

Regional planning body (RPB): Each of the English regions outside London has an unelected regional chamber. They are responsible for developing and coordinating the strategic planning policies for their region. The assembly is responsible for setting priorities and preparing regional spatial strategies, which determine, amongst other things, the number of new houses and where, in quite precise terms, they to be are built. This is in the regional housing strategy (RHS) which is, therefore in real terms, effectively controlled by central government.

Regional planning guidance (RPG): Regional planning policy and guidance issued for each region in England by the Secretary of State. Under the new system, the existing RPG becomes the regional spatial strategy for the region until formally revised by a replacement regional spatial strategy (RSS).

Renewable energy: A hot topic at present. Renewable energy occurs naturally and repeatedly in the environment, for example from the wind, water flow, tides or the sun without generating those evil carbon emissions.

Registered social landlord (RSL): A housing association or a not-for-profit company registered by the Housing Corporation to provide social housing.

Regularisation certificate: This is required for a retrospective approval under the building regulations of unauthorised work that has been carried out on or after November 11, 1985.

Repairs notice: Under the Planning (Listed Building & Conservation Areas) Act 1990, a council has power to serve such a notice on the owner of a listed building that is considered to be under threat. The notice sets out the repairs necessary to properly preserve the building. It can be an emergency repairs notice that seeks to prevent immediate damage by making the building wind and weather tight or it can be a full repairs notice with more extensive requirements.

Reserved matters: See Chapter 2.

Ribbon development: A longstanding phrase used to describe residential development that extends along one or both sides of a road from the edges of towns and villages into the countryside. It was one of the elements of urban sprawl that led to pressure for the control on where people should build that led to the planning acts in 1947.

Section 106 Agreement: A legal agreement under Section 106 of the 1990 Town & Country Planning Act. These are legal agreements between a planning authority and a developer, or they can take the form of unilateral undertakings offered by a developer, ensuring that certain extra works related to a development are undertaken. Section 106 Agreements deal with the provision of what has become known as planning gain. This is supposed to be no more than is required to provide the necessary social and physical infrastructure needed for a local place and its population to accommodate the new development without harm.

The advice on the use of Section 106 agreements is given in Circular 05/05 Planning Obligations. There are now moves afoot to greatly expand the amount of money extracted from developments through a planning gain supplement, which appears to be thinly veiled development land tax. If passed experience is anything to go by, it will simply act as a serious disincentive for landowners to release land for development.

Simplified planning zone: An area in which a local planning authority wishes to stimulate development and encourage investment. It operates by granting a specified planning permission in the zone without the need for an application for planning permission and the payment of planning fees. A power that is only likely to be used in areas of severe economic decline.

Site of nature conservation importance or site of biological interest: These phrases, and others like them, are used to signify non-statutory, but locally important, sites of nature conservation interest that have been identified by local authorities and that they wish to take account of in planning decisions.

Site of special scientific interest (SSSI): A site identified under the Wildlife and Countryside Act 1981 (as amended by the Countryside and Rights of Way Act 2000) as an area of special interest by reason of any of its flora, fauna, geological or physiographical features.

Sites and monuments record list: A publicly available description and assessment of all known ancient monuments and sites of archaeological interest in an area, including a map of each site.

Social inclusion: A concept of action taken by the state to try and include all sectors of society in planning and other decision-making processes – regardless of whether they are actually interested or not.

Social housing: Also described as Affordable Housing, this refers to housing which is cheaper than available on the open market. It is defined for the purposes of development plan policies in PPS 3 Housing, as follows: 'Affordable housing includes social rented and intermediate housing, provided to specified eligible households whose needs are not met by the market'. Social rented housing is: 'Rented housing owned and managed by local authorities and registered social landlords, for which guideline target rents are determined through the national rent regime'. Intermediate affordable housing is: 'Housing at prices and rents above those of social rent, but below market price or rents, and which meet the criteria set out above'.

Spot listing: The process by which buildings are listed on an individual basis in a hurry, often in response to an impending threat to a building due to a change in ownership or in response to a third-party request.

Statutory period: The time period (eight weeks for most minor applications and 13 weeks for major proposals) within which a local planning authority is required to make a decision on a planning application. If the period is exceeded, the applicant is entitled to consider the application as being refused and appeal to the Secretary of State against a deemed refusal. Local authorities tend to be slaves to these target dates as their performance is measured by the government in relation to them. These targets have the very undesirable effect of preventing negotiations during the consideration of a planning application. So, even though you may have reached agreement on changes, the local authority would rather refuse an application than miss their statutory period. If a Section 106 Agreement takes longer than expected, even if it is wholly the local authority's doing, they will refuse an application rather than hang on a few days to issue an approval. The net result is statistics that appear to show how fast the system is working but in reality it is slower and more expensive.

VI

Statement of community involvement (SCI): Sets out the processes and methods to be used by a local authority in carrying out local consultations and involving the community in the preparation and review of all local development documents and in the processing of planning applications. The statement of community involvement is an essential part of the local development framework and is, for obvious reasons, normally one of the first documents to be produced.

Statutory body/consultee: This refers to organisations that the local authority must consult as part of a planning application. It can include different bodies depending upon the nature and location of the particular proposal. Examples of such statutory bodies include Countryside Agency, English Heritage, Natural England, Environment Agency, Health & Safety Executive, Regional Development Agency and Sport England.

Statutory undertakers/statutory utilities: They may either be in public or private ownership such as Post Office, Civil Aviation Authority, Environment Agency or any water undertaker, any public gas transporters, supply of electricity etc. What they have in common is that they are bodies carrying out functions of a public service or infrastructure nature under a statutory power and have special dispensation to do things without needing to apply for planning permission.

Structure plan: The county's legal strategic planning policy document that was a key part of the old-style development plan. It sets out strategic planning policies that set the framework for the detailed policies in local plans. These plans are still around and will continue to operate in some areas for some until the regional spatial strategies and local development frameworks are finally finished.

Submission document: A development plan document that will be submitted to the Secretary of State for examination by an independent but government-appointed planning inspector.

Traffic calming: Traffic management measures specifically designed to reduce vehicle speeds along particular routes, normally used in residential areas, town centres and near schools. A sophisticated approach to traffic management in

which the pedestrian and cyclist take priority over the driver is the home zone. This includes traffic calming measures accompanied by more radical road narrowing, changes in surface materials and shared surfaces to achieve more pedestrian friendly residential roads. Traffic calming and home zones have the twin objectives of reducing accidents and improving the local environment.

Traffic/transport impact assessment: An assessment of the effects of a proposed development on the road network and highway safety, the assessment will normally include measures to deal with any adverse impact. It will often be expected to include a sustainability assessment of the availability of, and levels of access to, alternative forms of transportation.

Travel plan (sometimes called a green travel or commuter plan): There is an inherent conflict between our car-based economy and the public transport orientated planning system in which planners are constantly told to allow developments only in sustainable locations with access to alternatives to the private car. Because such locations are few and far between and most economically active people can afford a car, the green travel plan is a planning condition or Section 106 Agreement requirement that is attached to new commercial developments to make them seem more sustainable. Such travel plans aim to promote sustainable travel choices such as cycling or, more realistically, care sharing or home working.

Tree Preservation Order (TPO): The only mechanism available to local authorities to secure the preservation of single or groups of trees on the basis of their amenity value. A tree subject to a preservation order may not generally be topped, lopped or felled without the consent of the local planning authority. All local authorities have a statutory duty under the Town & Country Planning Act 1990 to consider protecting trees in the interest of local amenity. TPO's can protect individual or groups of trees or areas of woodland.

Unauthorised development: Development that has, or is, taking place without having had planning permission. Unauthorised, or unlawful development, may have taken place so long ago that no action can be taken against it. This is generally four years for built development and ten years for a change of use. If such development is quite recent it risks being the subject of enforcement action by the local planning authority.

Urban design: A discipline that is distinct from either architecture or planning that focuses upon the interaction between buildings and the spaces around them to create the places in which we mix and move, the public realm. Urban designers have an increasing role in putting together mixed-use development proposals to create pleasant places in which to live and work. Planners like to talk about good urban design and, just like high quality design, they often have difficulty in explaining exactly what they mean.

Urban extension: Jargon to describe a development on the edge of the built up area.

Urban capacity study: An audit carried out by local planning authorities to establish just how many houses could, in an ideal world, be accommodated within their built up areas. This would include some employment sites, derelict land and even areas of large back gardens where additional houses could in theory be built. Urban capacity studies are part of the attempt to build 60 per cent of new houses on previously developed land. But they are limited in what they can achieve because so many of the sites may never actually be redeveloped or come forward within a predictable time period. The inclusion of a site within an urban capacity study can help it get planning permission but it is no guarantee.

Urban regeneration: A highly fashionable concept in which under used and derelict land and properties are brought back into productive and environmentally beneficial use for the good of a town or city. This has become the career of choice for an army of local and national quangos and special interest groups who spend a lot of time and public money trying to persuade companies to invest their money in problem locations. Key issues tend to be fragmented land ownership, contaminated land problems, ownership by statutory undertakers, inadequate infrastructure, local bureaucracy and planning obstacles that prevent economically viable developments.

Urgent works notice: Councils have powers under the Planning (Listed Building & Conservation Areas) Act 1990 to take direct action to undertake urgent works necessary for the preservation of unoccupied listed buildings and buildings in conservation areas. The costs can be recovered from the

owners, often by attaching a charge to the property so that, if it is sold, the council can recover the money spent. Such notices tend to be a last resort when dealing with very awkward or absent property owners.

Use classes order: The Town & Country Planning (Use Classes) Order 1987 (as amended) groups land uses into various classes for planning purposes. For example, business uses are known as B1, B2 & B8. Changes of use within classes do not generally require planning permission but changes between classes often do. Where changes of use do not require permission it is because this has been specifically allowed by the General Permitted Development Order 1995 (as amended).

Vernacular: A word used to describe the traditional-style architecture that local authorities tend to prefer. It means very little other than local, utilitarian building styles from the past. Most so-called vernacular architecture is actually just standard countrywide Victorian or Edwardian period style. Planners tend to ask for designs to be changed to reflect local vernacular when they are not quite sure what else to say.

Village envelope (development boundary, settlement boundary): A line drawn around a village, or part of a village and shown on the local plan proposal maps to indicate the extent of the built up area of that settlement. Within this area, new residential development may, in certain circumstances, take place and beyond which will be classified as open countryside.

Visibility splays: The areas each side of an access across which it is necessary to see to ensure highway safety. Such splays, sometimes called sight lines, are normally required by planning conditions attached to a planning permission. In cases where vision splays go across third party land, a site may well be incapable of development without the active agreement of that third party. This is a common cause of problems and results in a ransom strip in the hands of the owner of the required vision splay land.

White land: An old fashioned phrase that was used to indicate land that had, in planning terms, no specific allocation or designated policy designation. Seldom encountered these days.

Wildlife corridor: Strips or wedges of land (for example, along a stream or hedgerow) that may be conserved and managed for wildlife, ideally linking more extensive areas of natural habitat.

Windfall site: A development site that has not been specifically allocated for development in a development plan. It is literally an unexpected windfall contribution to the housing supply of a district or borough. Government advice is that local planning authorities should not rely on such sites when setting housing delivery targets because they are so difficult to predict.

World Heritage Site: A historically important site designated by the International Council on Monuments and Sites, for example Durham Cathedral and Stonehenge.

Written representations: The description of a planning appeal which is made in writing only with no public hearing or discussion. The independent planning inspector will usually visit the site accompanied by both the appellant and council planner but no discussion of the issues is permitted.

We are always looking to improve our books. If there is a word or piece of jargon that you would like to see covered in future editions of this book – or even posted at www.housebuildersupdate.co.uk – then please e-mail: info@ovolopublishing.co.uk

Planning updates

Planning is a constantly changing game and we'll be posting updates from time-to-time in the planning section at: www.housebuildersupdate.co.uk

We'd also like to hear from you! If you would like additional information on any aspect of planning please let us know and we will do our best to include it on the website or in future editions of this book. Please email: planning@housebuildersupdate.co.uk Unfortunately, we cannot give individual replies or comment on specific planning applications.